The Two Kinds of Decay

The Two Kinds
of Decay

SARAH MANGUSO

GRANTA

Granta Publications, 12 Addison Avenue,
London W11 4QR

First published in Great Britain by Granta Books 2011
First published in the US in 2008 by Farrar,
Straus and Giroux

A CIP catalogue record for this book is available from
the British Library.

1 3 5 7 9 10 8 6 4 2

ISBN 978 1 84708 308 1

Some names and details have been changed.

Designed by Gretchen Achilles

Offset by Avon DataSet, Bidford on Avon,
Warwickshire

Printed and bound in Great Britain by the MPG Books Group,
Bodmin, Cornwall

Acknowledgments

With sincere thanks to the MacDowell Colony and the Corporation of Yaddo for their gifts of time and space; to Catherine Corman, Lisa Selin Davis, Jennifer L. Knox, Julie Orringer, and Emily Senecal for their invaluable notes; to PJ Mark and Denise Oswald for their good faith.

With deepest gratitude to my doctors, nurses, parents, friends. To Adam, whose work sustains mine and whose love makes me brave. There were so many others. Thank you.

The Two Kinds of Decay

The Beginning

The disease has been in remission seven years. Now I can try to remember what happened. Not understand. Just remember.

For seven years I tried not to remember much because there was too much to remember, and I didn't want to fall any further behind with the events of my life. I still don't have a vegetable garden. I still haven't been to France. I have gone to bed with enough people that they seem like actual people now, but while I was going to bed with them I thought I was catching up. I am sorry. I had lost what seemed like a lot of time.

I waited seven years to forget just enough—so that when I tried to remember, I could do it thoroughly. There are only a few things to remember now, and the lost things are absolutely, comfortingly gone.

I wrote down some things while the disease was happening—there are notes from one hospital stay and a few notes from the sickest years—but it isn't much.

Sometimes I think the content of those days might not have finished happening. It might have begun then, in 1995, but I needed to save the rest of it until I was stronger.

The events that began in 1995 might keep happening to me as long as things can happen to me. Think of spacetime, through which heavenly bodies fly forever. They fly until they change into new forms, simpler forms, with ever fewer qualities and increasingly beautiful names.

There are names for things in spacetime that are nothing, for things that are less than nothing. White dwarfs, red giants, black holes, singularities.

But even then, in their less-than-nothing state, they keep happening.

Allegri

I sang in a choir and took good care of my throat, and when I caught a head cold in February 1995, during my junior year of college, I took tea and herbal lozenges.

I liked that our British choirmaster didn't accept a head cold as a valid excuse for missing a rehearsal.

We took our duties seriously, for in serving our duties to the Memorial Church we might achieve excellence, which many of us valued above the other virtues.

I sang second soprano and I wasn't fearless, so I chose only a few solo auditions per year. I sang the second soprano solo in Gregorio Allegri's "Miserere," a setting of Psalms 50 and 51.

The piece was composed in the 1630s and has nine parts and is sung by three choirs standing in different parts of the church. When we sang it, the plainsong choir stood in the balcony, the solo choir stood behind the choir screen, and the rest of the choir stood before the congregation.

At some point in the seventeenth century, it became forbidden to transcribe the music. The piece was allowed to be performed only in the Sistine Chapel on Wednesday and Friday of Holy Week. Writing it down or performing it elsewhere was punishable by excommunication.

For more than a hundred years, legend has it, the piece was performed only at those two services.

In 1771, the fourteen-year-old Wolfgang Amadeus Mozart visited Allegri's church. He had a notoriously accurate ear and was a quick transcriber. Later that day, he wrote the piece down entirely from memory, and that was the end of the secret "Miserere."

I nursed a cold for weeks, trying to stay well enough that I could perform the piece in Cambridge, Massachusetts, on Sunday, March 5, 1995.

Our choirmaster gave us his notes on Tuesday. He said the solo choir had performed very well, *especially the second soprano, for singing a part which is quite difficult to keep in tune and which holds the group together.* I wrote that down.

I'd kept the virus hidden in my blood for weeks. The next day I let myself get sick and prepared to let the head cold run its course.

Signs

I still had the cold over spring break. I woke up on Sunday morning and my feet were asleep. I was at my parents' house, and I'd stayed out late.

I walked down the hall to the bathroom and my feet stayed asleep.

When I splashed water on my face, I couldn't catch my breath, couldn't seem to hold it long enough. How long does it take to wash a face—two seconds?

My hands were tingling a little.

Still tingling, I finished packing, brought my bags downstairs, put them in the car, and sat in the passenger seat while my father drove the ten miles back to my college dorm.

The dorm's elevator went to the even floors only, so I rode to the eighth floor and slid the bags down a flight to my room, G-73.

I phoned my parents the next night, and the one after that, and told them I'd come down with some kind of bug that was making me feel tired. I walked stiff-legged and slowly, and I was still nearly drowning every time I washed my face. My feet were numb, and my hands were getting numb, too.

I was concerned I'd caught a strange illness, but I was more concerned that I looked drunk. I was staggering around, even to and from breakfast, and I felt people looking at me and thinking it might be time for an intervention.

On my fourth day back at school, I fell down in the courtyard. Then I went upstairs and called my mother and asked her if she'd pick me up at school and take me to the hospital near their house, the hospital where I'd been born.

She drove me home first. She said my father would meet us there, would drive back early from his office on the South Shore, and the three of us would go to the hospital together.

That's when I understood something might really be wrong with me.

I remember walking from the back door of the house to the driveway, with my mother clutching my right arm so I wouldn't stumble on the brick path, and asking, *What's wrong with me?*

My father said, very calmly, *I don't know, Sar, but at the hospital they will.*

His calmness is the reason I didn't cry until almost twelve hours later, once I was in Intensive Care, my blood already churning through a machine, when a nurse explained to me that if the strength of my diaphragm weakened five more pounds per square inch of air pressure, I'd be intubated through a hole in my neck.

Bad Blood

I was brought upstairs from Emergency to Intensive Care and given a treatment called *apheresis*.

From the Greek *aphairein*, to take away.

In the hematological context, apheresis is the process of separating blood into its components (red cells, white cells, platelets, plasma), removing the component that's sick, and reinfusing the rest of it, along with a suitable replacement for the sick part. The sick part of my blood was the plasma.

My nurse told me about a man she treated whose body manufactured too many platelets, enough to clot his blood right in his blood vessels. And so when his blood was separated, the extra platelets were removed and thrown away, and replaced with saline to make up the lost blood volume.

I thought his platelet-producing powers might have been made useful—if his extra platelets could flow out of him, through an apheresis centrifuge, and right into a hemophiliac.

But of course the man's genes might have been diseased, or he might have been infected by a secret virus, and his platelets might have given someone his disease, or worse. So they were just collected in a bag and thrown away.

My plasma was filled with an antibody that destroyed peripheral nerve cells, so it was thrown away, too.

My plasma was replaced more than fifty times, and the effects of the treatment lasted as long as the fresh plasma stayed clean of the antibodies, which for several months was only about two days.

The machine took four hours to clean my blood. I bled eight ounces into the centrifuge, then the machine spun the blood fast enough to separate it into four layers. My plasma flowed into a bag, then my cells were mixed with saline, synthetic albumin (a blood plasma protein), and fresh frozen plasma, which contained the other plasma proteins. That new mixture was reinfused. And then the machine withdrew another cup and did the same thing, and then another cup, and so on, until the new plasma occupied enough blood volume that it was no longer useful to withdraw and clean another cup.

The first twenty times or so, before I had a central line—a tube in my chest that provided easy access to my blood—my arm veins were used for blood collection and reinfusion.

I received direct injection, via tubing connected to a *cannula*, or hollow needle—no flexible catheters were inserted. I had to lie still so the needles didn't tear my veins. Fourteen-gauge needles were used, large enough to keep my healthy cells intact so they could be reinfused. There was one in each crook of my elbow—one to take blood out and one to put it back in.

It is not easy to lie still with a fourteen-gauge needle in each arm, for four hours, shaking with cold that doesn't go away no matter how many heated blankets are tucked over you. The cold comes from the inside.

By comparison, routine blood draws, which I had several times a day, are taken via twenty-gauge cannulae, and infant lines are usually twenty-four-gauge. Twelve-gauge and fourteen-gauge cannulae are the widest used and deliver fluid faster even than lines that go to the heart, and are also known as *wide bores* or *trauma lines*.

Over time, the blood draws felt good. My veins were always in the process of healing from multiple punctures, and the tiny twenty-gauge prick scratched the itch that comes when flesh heals.

I bled out two liters of plasma during each treatment, but I was always given back more than two liters of fluid to prevent dehydration. Two liters of albumin, about a quarter liter of fresh frozen plasma, and some saline. I let my bladder fill as full as I could, but sometimes I had to raise my hips so someone could slide a pan under them for me to piss into.

The nurses always congratulated me on my impressive bladder volume. I once pissed 900 cc. That was my record.

The waste bag hung on the side of the machine and filled slowly with my yellow plasma. Periodically I'd ask the nurse to hold up the bag so I could see how full it was. It felt warm, like a bag of soup. By the end of each treatment, the small empty part left at the top of the bag would be clouded with condensation from the almost hundred-degree fluid.

One day during the treatment I was hungry and ordered a plate of french fries from the cafeteria. They were delivered, and I ate them during the treatment. This was later on, after my arm veins had scarred and after I had a central line in my chest, which left my arms free to move.

After that treatment, the plasma in the waste bag was pale and cloudy. The nurse and I realized I'd digested the french fries as my blood was being cleaned, and that the lipids from the french fry grease had been digested, released into my plasma through my small intestine, and then bled out into the apheresis machine.

After we figured that out, I ate french fries every time my plasma was replaced. My nurse and I imagined that in the future, people would have their plasma replaced whenever they ate rich meals.

Apheresis did a good job of cleaning out the mess in my blood, but since it only removes the antibodies once they're secreted into the blood, and doesn't prevent the body from making more, apheresis wasn't a permanent solution to the problem of my disease.

Metaphors

My blood plasma had filled with poison made by my immune system. My immune system was trying to destroy my nervous system. It was a misperception that caused me a lot of trouble.

All autoimmune diseases invoke the metaphor of suicide. The body destroys itself from the inside.

I secreted poison into my blood. The poison was removed and replaced with other people's blood and with chemicals.

With my own blood in me, I couldn't feel, and I couldn't move, but with other people's blood in me, and with chemicals in me, I could do those things.

The new blood became mine as soon as it entered me. Or maybe it took a moment to mix with what was there. Or maybe it took an hour, or a day.

My blood came out dirty and went in clean. It came out hot and went in cold. It came out old and went in new.

And the new, cold, clean blood was better than the blood I made myself.

A Role Model

Five years earlier, when people visited the bookstore where I worked and asked for books for their graduating nieces, or for a trip to the beach, or for a plane ride, right away I would tell them to buy *Catch-22*.

I wore a tan apron with a green name tag on the right side. I asked slowly and clearly, *May I help you find something?*

I made eye contact with the customers, then walked them to the books they needed. Walking the customer was the important part. Just saying *That section's in the back, in front of Travel*, or pointing to Pets, which was behind Science, didn't result in sales as often as walking the customer to the very shelf, pulling the book from the shelf, and placing it in the customer's hand.

One day my supervisor asked me to stop recommending *Catch-22* to the customers and instead to recommend any of the new clothbound books stacked pyramid-style on the front table. Someone had bought *Catch-22* from me at the front register, then come in later that day and returned it at the back register. My supervisor said it was the third or fourth return of the same paperback copy, and it was getting shopworn.

. . .

One night in 1994, because I had to be somewhere else, my college boyfriend brought my copy of *Catch-22* to Joseph Heller's book signing and had Heller inscribe it to me.

My copy of the book was a cheap paperback, with a bent aqua-colored cover, but I hope that as he held the book in his hands, Heller hadn't wished I'd sprung for a clothbound copy of his new novel, whatever it was, and that he was happy I'd read his famous book so many times and that I'd loved it enough to send someone out to have it signed for me.

Six months later I received the diagnosis that would become the focus of my life, and Heller died four years after that— after a long, slow recovery from the same disease.

Names

The first doctor known to have observed cases of my disease was Jean Landry, in 1859. He saw that his patients initially began to feel numbness and paresthesia (abnormal sensations) in their feet.

In addition to the strange sensations and numbness, the patients' feet grew weak and then paralyzed. And the numbness and paralysis spread upward from the feet, up the legs, and then continued up the torso to the diaphragm. When the diaphragm muscles weakened to the point that the patient could no longer breathe, the patient died.

And so the first proper name of my disease was *Landry's ascending paralysis*.

In 1916, two more French doctors, Georges Guillain and Jean Alexandre Barré, studied several people with ascending paralysis and observed the key diagnostic abnormality of increased spinal fluid protein but normal cell count.

And so the second proper name of my disease was *Guillain-Barré syndrome*.

The pathology is now understood as the immune system's generation of antibodies targeting the peripheral nerves' myelin, their protective and conductive protein sheath.

Landry's paralysis came from nerves that had lost their myelin. And the protein in Guillain and Barré's spinal fluid was made of that stripped-off myelin.

The condition may resolve spontaneously, relapse and remiss indefinitely, or progress and terminate in death.

In 1998, after my first year of graduate school, I put on my MedicAlert bracelet. It's engraved:

TAKES PREDNISONE FOR
CHRONIC IDIOPATHIC
DEMYELINATING
POLYRADICULONEUROPATHY

Chronic idiopathic demyelinating polyradiculoneuropathy. CIDP. That's the shortest name for what's wrong with me. It's something like a chronic form of Guillain-Barré syndrome but not exactly, and there isn't a proper name for it yet.

Statistics

Approximately 80 percent of Guillain-Barré syndrome patients have a complete recovery, and about 10 percent recover with severe disability, though the death rate among patients is still about 2 to 3 percent even in the best intensive care units.

It's hard to project these data onto my disease, CIDP. My disease is similar to but not the same as having Guillain-Barré syndrome over and over again, with no time to recover between bouts.

Some believe the clinical difference between Guillain-Barré syndrome and CIDP is subjective—that my disease was CIDP because I was sick for years instead of just a few weeks. Sometimes I think I might just have had a particularly bad case of Guillain-Barré syndrome.

Of course I'd rather have the common disease that people know how to treat, but there were times that I cherished my rare disease for its irrefutable proof of my specialness.

For its proof that my death, the end of the disease, whenever and in whatever form it came, was going to be remarkable.

Causation

Was the CIDP a physical manifestation of a spiritual illness?

Did the medication trigger the depression, or did the depression trigger the CIDP?

What about those yogis who can lie down on a bed of nails, then arise, streaming blood, then stop the flow of blood from each wound individually with the power of their minds? Isn't frailty often a choice?

And if frailty is a choice, then isn't an autoimmune disease a semi-intentional suicide?

What came first, the suicidal depression or the suicidal autoimmune disease?

Did they happen independently of each other, or not?

Sometimes I think that in the real universe, I am born already in possession of my CIDP, my depression, my whole life and death, and the text of this book. That I'm incapable of making the events of my life happen—either because they've already happened, or because they're always happening, at every possible point in spacetime.

And then sometimes I think I've made everything happen, starting with making myself be born.

The Internship

When I was sixteen, I was a volunteer intern at the local hospital.

I was given a white coat and a clipboard and accompanied the medical students on their clinical rounds.

I scrubbed in and watched vascular and orthopedic surgeries not knowing that in the future I'd have both kinds.

For several weeks in the pathology labs, I made slides from tissue samples suspended in wax.

One day a doctor and I visited a patient who was deeply asleep. She was an old woman, and her name was Anna.

I held Anna in my arms as the doctor listened for her breaths through a stethoscope held to her back. She wasn't cold or waxy or lying in a pile of excrescence, so we spent a long time trying to find a pulse. She looked no older or frailer or sleepier than many of the other elderly patients.

When we were sure Anna had died, the respiratory specialist recorded the time as her time of death. Then the respiratory specialist and I went back to his office, and he told me it was all right to feel disturbed or upset by what had happened.

I didn't feel upset, but I thought I should, so I stared at the wall and tried to look solemn.

The respiratory specialist said I could sit in his office for the rest of the afternoon with a couple of interns who were doing his paperwork. And so all afternoon I sat and stared at the wall and looked solemn, and periodically one of the interns would ask me if I felt all right, and I would say, solemnly, *Yes*.

One night, five years later, in the same hospital, a woman came into my room to take blood. But it wasn't one of the phlebotomists. It was Louise, from the pathology lab, where I'd made slides from all those tissue samples all those years before!

I told her I'd been an intern in 1990, and that I'd liked working with her. She said she remembered me.

Blood and Shit

My shoulders still allowed my arms to rotate behind me, but my hands were too weak to resist even the slightest pressure. I couldn't wipe my ass.

It's hard to wipe someone else's ass. After asking for a few extra swipes, I'd feel embarrassed, and then I'd say to hell with it even though my ass would itch like hell later and I wouldn't have the strength to scratch it.

One of my nurses was a year younger than I was. She was the kind of person who would visit her brother and his family and see the house wasn't clean and then clean the entire house. And she really knew how to wipe an ass. With a washcloth soaked in hot water, and then with a dry towel.

I thanked her so profusely the first time that she was moved to explain. *I could wipe shit all day*, she said, smiling.

Even blood didn't bother her. *Blood is for life*, she'd said another time, when a line had popped out of my arm and I'd shot a blood geyser all over my bed.

I watched her clean up messes that horrified me, and she was cheerful, always.

One day she told me about the phlegm that formed in cancerous lungs. Sometimes she had to suction that phlegm. And sometimes it was black with necrotic tissue.

The young nurse said she'd never got used to the odor of that phlegm.

Sometimes I could hear people being suctioned. And sometimes above the slurping sound I heard the people yell in pain or in fear at seeing their own dead selves being sucked out of them.

The Wrong Symptom

The nerve damage associated with my disease is supposed to begin at the toes and move upward, as if you're sinking in invisible, numbing quicksand.

Or sometimes it begins at the hands and moves up the arms to the torso—as if you're standing in the quicksand on your hands.

During one of my hospitalizations, after being pricked with the pinwheel—a metal tool resembling a pizza cutter—I reported a spot of numbness on my abdomen. It was, coincidentally, about the size of a slice of pizza. The numb spot was surrounded by flesh that could feel. And that symptom wasn't clinically normal for someone with my disease.

There was no diagnostic explanation for that numb spot, and so the following explanation was given: while there may in fact be a symptomatic area on my abdomen, the symptom I was reporting was not the correct one.

In my disease, the numbness starts distally, in the toes and fingers, and progresses proximally, toward the trunk. In my disease, there are no numb spots on the trunk. Those neurons aren't stripped of their myelin until the arms and legs go numb first.

After considerable discussion among the doctors and their entourage of students, it was declared that I had indigestion, which was common in patients who had been lying on their backs for days or weeks as I had, and it was declared that since I was used to reporting all symptoms as numbness, I was feeling heartburn and reporting it as numbness.

If I broke a toe or lacerated my palm, it was apparently assumed I'd report the pain as numbness because I'd become accustomed to calling my discomfort *numbness.*

A doctor listened to my belly through his stethoscope and declared gastric unrest, though there is always some unrest in the bellies of the living.

I was prescribed a few tablespoons of liquid antacid. I drank it and the symptom abated a little, maybe.

And so the sensory changes had been caused, of course, by the antacid, just as the symptom had been caused by indigestion, and just as the indigestion had been caused by my having lain on my back for so long.

But not really.

Bananas

The next time you have some sensory nerve damage, touch the paresthetic skin and evaluate its numbness.

Wait a minute. Then touch the skin again.

Wait another minute, then touch it again. Again. Wait an hour. Two hours, ten hours, a day, two days.

Is the numbness changing? Getting bigger, smaller, stronger, weaker? What have you done in the last four days? Sometimes potassium deficiency causes paresthesia. Have you eaten many bananas in the last four days? Go to the store and buy six bananas and eat them in the space of a morning. And feel that, yes, the numbness is disappearing! Since digesting most of the six bananas, your hands now feel a softer version of the soft quilt you have been lying under!

The world, with its infinite variables, is the wrong place to attempt implementing the scientific method. Most successful experiments work only in vacuums. Boyle's law, Newtonian mechanics—only in vacuums are they true.

Narratives in which one thing follows from the previous thing are usually imaginary.

Everything that happens, happens in a moment that follows from all the other moments in spacetime.

As I see it, that's the main problem with neurological symptoms that can't be measured in numbers yet, and why many of my symptoms weren't treated.

Those symptoms weren't treated because they were unlikely enough to be virtually impossible. My reports of them were their only observable evidence.

My symptoms were so unlikely, by the book, that despite my reports of them, they were assumed not to exist.

Strength

After my first hospitalization I was sent home with a prescription for three physical therapy sessions per week at the local rehabilitation center. I was all better.

My physical therapist asked me what I wanted to be able to do, and I tried to think of the hardest thing I'd been able to do before I'd got sick. I said *run three miles*.

The therapist knew how to strengthen each muscle that had been weakened by the rogue antibodies in my blood, and she took a few minutes to record the strength of each muscle and to write a detailed plan, and then she explained the plan to me.

All I remember of her plan is that she pronounced the word *strength* as *shtrenth*. Over and over.

I got on the treadmill, but I had foot drop—my feet slapped down because I was too weak to dorsiflex, to turn my ankle and toes upward—and so I stomped with flat feet. Marched. And tripped a lot. I was going one mile per hour. The first day, I walked for five minutes. Eighty-three thousandths of a mile.

I stayed on the young therapist's rehabilitation plan for one week, getting weaker instead of stronger, and then, eleven days after being discharged, I wound up back in the hospital.

I did eventually run three miles, but it took nine years.

The First Time

Unused to being frail, I returned to college and stayed up very late that first night reading mail and writing papers and cleaning out the refrigerator, and in the morning I lay in bed vomiting into the wastepaper basket from fatigue, and less than two weeks later I was back in the hospital.

The Hematologist

My disease has two steps: the immune system secretes anti-bodies into the blood. Then the blood delivers the antibodies to the peripheral neurons.

The antibodies destroy the neurons. First they eat away the cells' myelin sheaths, then they eat away the cells themselves, which heal more slowly, if at all.

And so I had a nerve doctor and a blood doctor.

The stereotype for hematology/oncology specialists, or hem-oncs (pronounced almost like *he-monks*)? They are the self-styled St. Judes, patrons of useless causes.

My hem-onc was special. He was from Norway. And he didn't mind sitting in my wheelchair if it were nearer my bed than the armchair.

He told me that he and one of his terminal patients played a game every day he visited the patient at the hospice. The hem-onc brought music recordings with him, and he'd try to stump the terminal patient, who knew a lot about classical music. Like, with the slow movement of one of the less famous of Mozart's piano sonatas. And the terminal patient, who had a lot of records with him, would usually guess correctly what the piece was, and then he would try to stump the hem-onc.

The hem-onc visited his terminal patient first thing in the morning, then visited me, and then saw the rest of his patients.

He had a daughter about my age, and their relationship was not good, and it troubled him. She was a lesbian, and he didn't know how to talk to a teenaged lesbian daughter.

Talking to me was easy for him. He knew how to talk to people with blood diseases.

One day he told me his terminal patient, the one with all the classical records, had died.

How many other terminal patients did he have? How many deaths had my hem-onc witnessed? Did he feel like a failure when his patients died? And by that metric, what case isn't a failure, in the end?

What metric is used instead of immortality to judge the success of a hem-onc?

The Sikh

My first central line was implanted in the middle of the night. I needed apheresis right away, and my arm veins were finally blown. That's a clinical term. They had scarred and narrowed. I still have my tracks. I should have been given a central line earlier, but every apheresis session was declared the last one I'd ever need, so it was a while before anyone noticed it was time to get serious.

Central lines flow through a catheter into a large vein, usually the vena cava. Central lines can deliver more toxic fluids that would irritate smaller veins, and they have room to contain multiple lumens, and they can deliver fluids faster, as the heart distributes them immediately.

My hematologist asked me if I wanted my parents there while it was implanted, and though I'd never have thought of bothering them in the middle of the night, I thought he was telling me that getting a central line was something that one's parents were supposed to be there for, so I said *sure*. And so my parents came to watch me get my first central line implanted.

My hematologist might have thought I'd wanted my parents there to help me feel less fearful, but I didn't know enough about the procedure to feel fearful. Yet I was old enough to have known that watching their child have vascular surgery isn't something parents should do.

I didn't have to watch. I was on my back, and the Sikh doctor, who attached his surgical mask behind his head with a bent paper clip, as the tops of his ears were tucked under his white turban, jabbed away at my subclavian vein.

I'd been told I'd be injected with lidocaine, and that a needle would be stuck into my subclavian vein at a point just below my collarbone, and that while the needle was in the vein, a tube would be threaded over it and pushed down, through my skin, and through the hole in the vein, and deep into the vein, over the needle, and that the tube would be taped (and later sewn) to my skin, and that the needle would then be withdrawn, leaving the tube in place.

What if I'd been told someone would be standing over me, massaging my collarbone, while I lay blindfolded? That's something I would have tolerated. And up to the point that the lidocaine began to wear off, that's almost what it felt like.

If the procedure had lasted only a couple of minutes, I might have been all right.

But the doctor flubbed the procedure. He kept getting the needle in, but he couldn't jam the tube over it. The entry angle was too sharp.

So the lidocaine began to wear off, and the doctor kept telling the interns and the surgery residents exactly what the trouble was, and he became frustrated when he couldn't get the tube into me, and tried another, thinner tube, and sweated onto me, and stunk up the entire room with his frustration.

He tried again and again to jam the tube into my vein. Every now and then he had to stop and apply pressure, as I was bleeding. At one point I thought I felt a jet of blood spurt into my chest cavity, and that's when I lost my composure.

Months later, after his hair had gone from steel gray to white, my father told me it had looked like a horror movie.

The Taste

The fresh frozen plasma was thawed before it was infused. The four half-liter glass bottles of albumin were left at room temperature.

For the first twenty or thirty apheresis sessions, I lay under several blankets, which didn't help the cold but helped me think at least I was trying.

The temperature in blood vessels is warmer than room temperature, of course, by about thirty degrees Fahrenheit. I was very slowly infused with several liters of fluid that was thirty degrees colder than the rest of my body.

By the time I had the permanent line, the cold infusions went in very close to my heart. I need to describe that feeling, make a reader stop reading for a moment and think, *Now I understand how cold it felt.*

But I'm just going to say it felt like liquid, thirty degrees colder than my body, being infused slowly but directly into my heart, for four hours.

The albumin had a taste. To be more specific, the albumin had two tastes, because the hospital bought albumin from two different manufacturers.

Both companies used the same 500 cc clear glass bottles, which were sealed at the narrow end with rubber drums that could be sterilized and punctured with sterile needles and connected to sterile tubing.

One company's albumin was the color of light beer and the other company's was the color of lager. And the dark albumin tasted worse.

I never could decide whether it was *chemical* bad or *organic* bad.

I had to taste it for three or four hours, unabatedly, and there was nothing I could do to change the taste of it. It wasn't touching the surface of my tongue, but it was going into the blood in my heart, which pumped it into every cell in my body. It was *in* my tongue.

The only thing that masked the taste of the albumin was wintergreen-flavored candy.

Tabitha, my favorite apheresis nurse, always arrived with a bag of wintergreen candies, individually wrapped. She picked them out of the mix for me—there were red and yellow and purple candies, too, and different kinds of mint—and left a small pile of them behind, because the taste of the albumin lasted for a while after the infusion was over, and she wanted to make sure

I had enough wintergreen to get through the rest of the day without having to taste any albumin. Without that reminder of how I'd spent the morning.

The Cheerleader

I attended a public school with cheerleaders, pep rallies, and powder-puff football. My high school's mascot was the Red Raider, and he was represented by an American Indian wearing a headdress and waving a tomahawk.

One day every fall, just before Thanksgiving, the principal would remind us over the public address system that today was the biggest pep rally of the year and that our school needed us to show our spirit.

By *school* he meant *varsity football team*. Our football team's rivalry with that of an adjacent town was the oldest high school football rivalry in the United States of America, and there was an engraved monument downtown, in front of the police station, to remind us.

When I was a freshman, I went to the pep rally. I hadn't figured out yet that as long as I got good grades, no one would care if I spent two entire semesters of Spanish in the photography darkroom, or if I left school after sixth period to hang out downtown at Coffee Connection.

At the pep rally the principal introduced the football coach, and the football coach introduced each team member individually, and everyone in the bleachers cheered when each player entered the gymnasium from one end and walked across to the other, where the coach was standing with his megaphone.

The football players were shirtless, their muscular chests painted with red "war paint," and they swaggered as if they'd taken the virginity of half the girls in the sophomore class, which they had.

And all the women in the whole senior class, even the fat and ugly and unpopular ones, wore red felt dresses they had made, with scissor-cut fringe and matching red felt headbands decorated with white feathers, and they wore red "war paint" on their faces, too, because they were the Senior Squaws. And they were addressed by the football coach and saluted for their great spirit and for their help to the cause at hand, which was to beat Needham.

The cheerleaders cartwheeled in their red and white and black regulation skintight uniforms in rows across the gym, then danced like strippers to bass-pumping music. They jumped and flashed their asses, and at the end there was a pyramid, and then more screaming, after which the football coach congratulated the young women on their display of talent and skill.

In a yearbook photo of this very pep rally, I am sitting in the bleachers with my friend who dropped out to go to art school, and the two of us look stoned. All around us are blurry teenagers, their faces just sharp enough to broadcast their ecstasy.

At the powder-puff football game the Senior Squaws wrestled in the mud and were very drunk. It was summarized, in code, in the *Senior Voice*, the underground newspaper for seniors, which detailed the events of their last month in high school, the month of spirit days (Hat Day! Shaving Cream Day!), and which was very easy to find lying around the cafeteria every morning.

Seven years later, I was in the hospital, too nauseated to eat. I was too nauseated not just to eat but to swallow even a sip of water.

I was prescribed a strong antiemetic. In suppository form. And the nurse who pushed it into my ass had been one of the varsity cheerleaders from that 1988 pep rally.

Like all good nurses, she understood that inserting a bullet of hardened gel into someone's rectum was just another thing that had to be done, no more or less willingly than picking up a dropped rubber glove or stripping a bed after someone died in it.

She radiated love without smiling. And when she finished her shift at seven that night, she sat with me, still in her tight white uniform, and we watched *Dirty Dancing* on television, talking a little during the commercials.

That's what she was like.

The Forgetful Nurse

She worked the morning shift and she understood slow, simple English. Every morning she came in to help me to the bathroom, and she grabbed my arm at the biceps and yanked it up. And every day she did that, I cried out because it hurt a little and because I knew that if the tube in my chest were pulled out, I would bleed out. I wouldn't bleed to death, but I'd probably fall down, and she wouldn't be able to pick me up to see where the blood was coming from, and I'd pass out from fright and blood loss, and eventually the wound would be found and pressure would be applied, but not before I'd bled out enough to cause myself even more trouble.

Every day, after that happened, and after I got back from the bathroom, she gave me a sponge bath and toweled me off. Since I wasn't wearing a hospital johnny and the line in my chest was exposed, I wasn't afraid she would knock it out of the vein or pull it out by accident.

But then she always took out a little container of baby powder and started shaking it onto my torso. And I had been reminded by the surgeons, every time one of them implanted a line, that nothing powdery should be used near the entry site, because the powder could get right into my bloodstream.

So then I reminded her, my voice raised, to keep the powder away from my line.

And both of those things happened every day she worked.

The New Machine

A new apheresis machine was delivered to the hospital. It was the manufacturer's prototype. The company had sent it out for human trials.

This machine worked faster than the old one. Instead of withdrawing a cup of blood, cleaning it, and reinfusing it, the new machine withdrew and reinfused my blood continuously. And it could reinfuse at a faster clip because it had a built-in blood warmer. There would be no chills, no shaking.

I was the first human to use that machine.

The day the machine was delivered, Tabitha hooked me up to the albumin, gave me a wintergreen candy, and told me an engineer was coming to talk with me—one of the engineers who had designed the new machine.

She brought him upstairs and left us alone. For a moment, he just looked at me, connected to the machine he had helped invent, and I just looked at him. I was happy to be able to shake his hand, as I was using a central line and my arms were free to bend at the elbow.

He asked me how the machine felt, and I told him how good it felt to have a blood warmer, how I would miss it if I had to go back to using the old machine. I told him how good it was to know that the treatment would last two hours instead of four.

And I told him what it was like to arrive at the hospital with paralyzed legs and then to have six or seven treatments over six or seven days, using an apheresis machine made by his company, and then to walk out of the hospital on my own legs, my arms held out a little for balance.

He tried not to smile, but he smiled. I hope he felt proud. He had made something good, and it had helped me. And he had seen it—seen the moment his invention worked.

We talked about my college studies, and about his work, and about his volunteer work with the Boys Club of America. He stayed with me until a half hour was left in the treatment and then said he would go and find Tabitha. She needed to disconnect the last of the four bottles of albumin that had emptied into me, and to disconnect me from the machine, and to seal and remove the four-liter bag of my dirty plasma. Tabitha came back and did all the things she needed to do. The engineer said goodbye.

But he returned, with a bouquet of flowers.

Paralyzed

A spinal cord injury can paralyze you in a moment, but the paralysis of my disease is a long story. Worse, then better, then worse, then better. For years.

A woman rides her motorized chair up a ramp and onto a stage. Ten feet away from the podium, she parks her chair, gets up, and walks a few steps, very slowly, to accept her award.

What a sickening prop.

But people forget a woman in a chair is strong enough to walk a few steps each day and has saved this day's steps for the acceptance of her award.

Chair or no chair: a binary relation. But the vicissitudes of moving the body around are infinite. You never know what a person in a chair can do.

I saw two young women at a lecture once, one of them in a wheelchair that looked like a piece of expensive Italian furniture. Her girlfriend sat down and said *You want to do a transfer?*

and the girl in the chair said *Yeah* and maneuvered her chair next to the bank of auditorium seats, placed her hands on the arms of the first seat, and swung herself into it with her ropy upper body. Then she reached over and folded up her hot little wheelchair.

Other than the ones I used in the hospital, I never got my own chair. When I couldn't walk I stayed in bed, because it was always assumed I'd get better soon, and the chair was for people who were done forever with walking.

I was afraid of the chair. It would indicate I wasn't going to get better. And my doctors didn't want to believe that any more than I did.

Chair or no chair: a binary relation. Bad or good, sick or well, hopeless or hopeful.

This is how I described paralysis to my friends: *Sit down right next to me on a bench or a sofa, me on the left, our four thighs in a row. Lift your right thigh and put it back down. Then the next thigh over, lift it and put it down. Then the next thigh after that.*

That feeling of trying to lift someone else's thigh with your own mind is how it feels to be paralyzed.

Though my worst relapse paralyzed me from the thighs down and weakened me everywhere else, most of my paralysis was always in the process of getting either better or worse. The state of my health changed daily.

During a week of plasma exchanges, I'd be able to move a little more each day. That's how quickly the myelin regrew. If I were waiting at home to get sick enough to be readmitted to the hospital, I'd be able to move a little less each day. That's how quickly the myelin was destroyed by my anxious blood.

My feet were often completely paralyzed, because they'd go first and weaken the most. To this day, scratching my arches, even lightly, is excruciating, but the toes and the rest of the sole can take pins. There was some permanent damage, either to the axons or to the myelin or both. Now my feet are both hypersensitive and hyposensitive.

I was always being moved around, given physical therapy and having my bedsheets changed under me, so most of the big parts of my body got at least a little movement each day.

But the toes, when one is lying down, do not get a lot of attention. After a week or more with paralyzed feet, my toes needed to be moved right away. I couldn't bear the stillness anymore. It was like a full bladder. When my parents visited that afternoon, I asked my father to move my toes. He grasped one set of toes in each hand and bent them up and down and all around in a bunch for a few minutes. And either he or my mother did this every day they visited until I was strong enough to sit up and reach my toes myself.

Death

When I told my hematologist I was worried about dying, he smiled and said, *Look, here is the smallest violinist in the world playing you a Dvořák violin concerto*, as he rubbed his index finger against his thumb.

A cancer patient on the ward, a girl a year or two older than I was, had a catheter just like mine, except tiny. Like the thickness of a piece of angel hair pasta instead of the thickness of two drinking straws with big clamps at the ends. And that little piece of pasta could be rolled up and sealed under a plastic patch, and that girl could go swimming.

And she did—in the ocean, on Cape Cod. And got a blood infection, because she had leukemia.

But our hem-onc didn't tell me she was a nuisance for having ruined her catheter and for having made the surgeon implant a new one, and our hem-onc didn't tell me the girl was dying, or that he had wanted her to swim again before she died.

He didn't say it, but I am pretty sure he told her to go to the ocean and get in it and let the water go above the access site, and that if the briny water leaked through the adhesive around the edges of the plastic patch, to stay in the water and swim until she was tired of swimming.

Our hem-onc just told me she had swum in the ocean with her catheter, and that she had got it infected. And he smiled the way we do when we talk about naughty affairs or petty crimes that people get away with.

The fear of death came once, and that was it. It was like getting an immunity to the chicken pox. It never goes away. I am learning not to remember it.

The first time I was brave. I kept grief at bay for a long time. The moment I gave up, then everything—horror, grief, all of it—came in a great rush.

Every other time, I fell into it as if into a soft mat. I yielded instantly, thinking *It is here again, this certainty I will soon die, this thing I already know that I have not forgotten for a single minute.*

Cavities

One day, while I was mostly paralyzed and my muscles were atrophying repulsively, two nurses scooped me up into a hammock attached to a scale and told me how much I weighed.

I'm half an inch shy of six feet, and in the hammock I weighed a hundred and ten pounds, and that wasn't even my skinniest.

People brought me rich foods to eat, but there was no point. Extra food would turn to fat in me, as I couldn't move to stimulate any muscle growth.

And the fatter I got, the harder it got for my muscles to move my body.

Not all of the nurses understood this. Particularly not the tubbier ones.

Still, I wasn't avoiding rich foods. I ate french fries all day. I ate as much as I wanted, which still wasn't much.

I did care about my teeth, though. Having my teeth drilled seemed an avoidable inconvenience.

And so at night, after my teeth had been brushed, when I was offered a cup of soda for my bedside table, I always asked for diet instead of regular.

And sometimes I got the look. The look that says *Oh you goddamned malingering brat, starving yourself to get attention while in the next room there are people dying.*

For a while I explained that it was to keep from getting cavities, as I was unable to manipulate a toothbrush to clean my own teeth after drinking a syrupy sugar drink, but then I gave up because of course an anorectic would say that.

Corticosteroids, which I took for a long time, eat away at the skeleton, and it's not uncommon for the teeth to rot a little. And that's not even taking into consideration that my teeth weren't being brushed very regularly or very well.

But it's been twelve years since my diagnosis, and I still don't have a single cavity.

Hair

I did lose some hair, but no clumps. Or none that I noticed. Then again, I was too weak to lift my arms to touch my head, and my fingers were more or less paralyzed, and all the little muscles in my hands had atrophied. The pillows of flesh that had been on my palms, at the base of each thumb, had withered.

And so the nurses washed my hair for me. But washing a patient's hair is a lower priority than reconnecting a line that has been pulled out of a vein by accident or on purpose, or defibrillating a heart that has arrested, so I didn't ask for a shampoo very often.

When my college boyfriend came to visit me for the first time, he declared my condition *greasy but stable.*

After eight or ten days, a nurse would wash my hair for me, whether I'd asked her to or not. If I were paralyzed, this involved transferring me from my bed to a wheelchair, wrapping my central line in waterproof plastic, wheeling me into the shower, sticking my head into the stream of water, doing three or four shampooings, soaking the entire room, and pulling out what looked like pounds of my dead hair.

Sometimes a nurse wouldn't want to deal with cleaning up such a mess, and she would wheel me down the hall to a rinsing sink, above which hung a sign that said something to the effect that it was not for patients' use. But the rinsing sink was the perfect height for washing a slumped, paralyzed girl's hair.

One nurse would wash my hair while another stood watch. Sometimes we got in trouble, but it was worth it. All the nurses had to do after washing my hair in the rinsing sink was to wipe it with a couple of towels, fold them so no one could see they were filled with hair, and throw them down the laundry chute.

God knows, the anorectics threw worse things down there.

Tests

First you'll feel a tiny sting where the needle goes into the lumbar spine, then a small burn when the anesthetic is pushed into the tissue, then a bit of pressure when the second needle goes in, and then nothing. You'll just lie there on your side, fetal, and if an intern or a student gets to do the puncture, you'll hear everyone congratulate the intern or the student once the fluid is in the test tube. And if you ask to see your spinal fluid, someone will hold up a test tube of perfectly clear fluid.

And then everyone's happy and you'll just lie flat awhile until there's no risk you'll get the notorious spinal-tap headache if you move.

You can rest knowing it will be days before you'll hear whether the fluid contains a high protein content yet a normal cell count, the combination of which indicates severe nerve damage.

These days, hospitals have open MRI machines, but my hospital had only the closed kind. If you needed an MRI taken of the top of your neck, you were slid all the way inside the machine.

Once you're inside, it's hard not to notice that the wall of the hollow tube is no more than six inches away from your body at any point.

My muscles were atrophied when I had my MRIs, and I was very thin. If the walls had been only six inches away from my body, a larger person wouldn't have been able to fit into the machine. So this memory must not be right.

But the point is that once you're inside, if you have any imagination at all, you feel as if you have been buried alive in a white plastic coffin.

This is why MRI technicians offer a slight sedative before the procedure, and why they say to keep your eyes shut and imagine that the thudding sounds of the machine are waves crashing on a beach, and why they speak to you throughout the test, asking how you're feeling and declaring that you're doing well, and why they place a panic button in your right hand. If you press it at any point, they slide you right out of the tube.

If you think you might open your eyes inside the tube, ask for a washcloth to be laid over your eyes. It will work as a blindfold, even if you open your eyes underneath it, and since you're in a coffin, you can't move your arms or any other part of your body to touch the blindfold, and you will not be afraid.

More Tests

For a nerve conduction velocity test, electrodes are stuck to the skin above the tips of the neuron in question. Then electric shocks are delivered directly to the nerve cells. You lie there and get shocked. You know the shocks are coming. It's simple.

The shocks start small and get bigger. There is a break of one second between one shock and the next.

For the first few series of shocks, you think it wasn't so bad. Even the strongest shock isn't enough to make your whole body seize. If it's a leg nerve that gets shocked, the biggest shocks will only make your leg thrash.

That's the whole first part. It lasts an hour or less to test three or four nerves. And while the discomfort is unrelenting, the pain is not excruciating.

An electromyogram is more or less the same—electrodes delivering shocks—but with sensor needles in the muscles that those nerves innervate. So it's the same shocks, but you must keep the muscle tense while the shocks are delivered to the nerve cells and while a needle is jutting out of the muscle.

The technicians always ask whether it's your first EMG. If it is, they say it's all right to cry. And maybe they'll add that men cry more than women, or that a great big juiced-up guy from South Boston is more likely to cry than a librarian from North Cambridge. Or that people who try hard not to cry are more likely to cry than people who are open to the possibility that they might cry. The EMG technicians watch people get tortured all day, but it is hard even for them to guess how anyone will hold up until the actual breaking point.

I got through my first three EMGs without crying. Each one got easier.

But then one day, when there were no lab technicians available, a doctor administered my EMG. He could deliver the test as well as interpret the results, right there, while the data from the first shocks showed on the computer screen.

And I asked him what the data looked like, and he said the data looked bad. My nerves' conduction velocities were slower than they'd been the last time, and their conduction block had increased. The antibodies had destroyed more myelin.

And right away I knew I would need to get a new central line implanted and have my plasma replaced again, and I also knew that each time the myelin was stripped from my nerves, it was likelier to grow back imperfectly, and that I was likelier to lose strength and sensation permanently.

It wasn't the EMG but the bad news that made me cry. It's probably best to have an EMG while someone's opening your mail and finding that you got into college, or while you're watching the right lottery numbers appear on the television screen.

If you start crying during an EMG, you can pretty much forget about trying to stop crying until the test is over.

I'd guess that if you get a dozen EMGs in your life, it's likely you'll cry during at least one of them.

I don't know any other hospital procedure that makes people cry as reliably as an EMG except the test of the blood's clotting agents, when you just sit and bleed from a puncture wound, and the blood drips until your fibrinogens and platelets create a barrier to the bleeding, or it's decided you've lost enough blood that it's certain your fibrinogens and platelets aren't going to be able to stop the blood, and then the test is over.

Tabitha

Tabitha called nail polish *nail enamel*. Her daughter was ten or fifteen years older than I was. The daughter had lived out of her car for a long time.

Rock and roll, I said after Tabitha told me that. Living out of your car was cool. It wasn't even her car. It was her boyfriend's car.

Tabitha never scolded me for saying stupid things. She told me her daughter had a skin-picking problem. Lesions on her face.

Lesions?

Just acne. Small inflammations. Tabitha liked using the proper medical terms for things. She told me the story of her first day of nursing school. She'd already read the text for the week ahead, and when the professor asked what *p.o.* meant in a clinical context, Tabitha said she raised her hand and said *per os*, by mouth, as if it were nothing at all. Rock and roll.

Tabitha manipulated the hell out of that apheresis machine. I hardly shook.

When my line stopped delivering blood to or from my heart, and the machine's alarm rang, Tabitha twiddled with the pump until my blood flowed again. The other apheresis nurses moved my body around, unwrapped me from my cocoon of heated blankets, and twisted the tubes around like secretaries playing with telephone cords.

The worst nurses injected heparin, which was the fastest solution of all—nothing makes blood flow like a shot of blood thinner.

But Tabitha knew that even when you're sick, when you no longer mind things that once horrified you, avoiding even one unnecessary subcutaneous injection can put you in a better mood.

Tabitha knew that machine, and she knew my heart—she could infuse anything into it, and I'd scarcely notice. And she brought those wintergreen candies with her as if it were part of my prescription.

Besides her daughter she only ever mentioned a deadbeat ex-husband who'd abandoned her.

Walking

I returned to school after the first couple of hospitalizations, and both times I made appointments with the disabilities office.

A van would pick me up and take me to and from my classes and wherever else I had to go. The van was driven by a student, and it was free, and it never came when I needed it. I seldom went to class, and when I did, I was late.

The driver helped me into the van even though it wasn't in her job description and she knew I could sue her if I were injured while entering or exiting the van. Since she got in trouble for being late, she helped me. I took too long to drag my body up the van's three steps on my own.

At that point I was using two crutches. Crutches weren't a good solution to my mobility problem, generalized limb weakness that worsened distally.

I wasn't safely mobile on the crutches. I shouldn't have gone back to school. My doctors were doing the best they could, but they must have been delusional to think it was safe to let me go back to Cambridge without a wheelchair. I was still poisoning myself a little more with every beat of my heart, barely able to manipulate my crutches, just waiting until I wasn't able to manipulate the crutches at all.

I remember walking out of Adams House one night, after dinner with a friend, barely able to stand upright, crutches splayed out to the sides. Someone behind me said something. I realized my crutches were blocking the entire patio, from brick wall to brick wall, and that no one could walk past me. And of course I was walking very slowly. And of course I was not doing what properly could be called walking. I was slumped over the crutches, which were braced against the walls.

The brick walls were all that was holding me up.

My friend carried me the rest of the way down the slate patio and onto the sidewalk and into the van.

Rehabilitation

My third hospitalization was fourteen days instead of the usual ten because the covering neurologist didn't schedule my five plasma exchanges right away. I had to wait a day or two before each one, and during those days the antibodies ate away at my nerve cells. By the end of the hospitalization I could breathe, but I still couldn't walk.

And so on May 26, 1995, the last day of my longest hospitalization, it was decided I would move to a rehabilitation hospital where I'd learn to walk and use my hands again.

My parents had already been to my college dorm and packed everything and brought it home. Somewhere in there was a small pipe and a few extra screens and a film canister full of marijuana buds.

They drove me to a northern Massachusetts town none of us had ever been to.

I was admitted and shown my room, which I would share with an old woman who coughed and whose medications and preparations filled our bathroom.

I had a bed, a night table, and a chair. There was a window I could look out of. Outside was Massachusetts.

A nurse came in to take my temperature with one of the new infrared ear thermometers that no one knew how to use yet.

She reported my body temperature as eighty-two degrees Fahrenheit.

I suggested that that was not possible since I was still living.

She took my temperature several more times and eventually recorded it as ninety-two degrees.

My parents and I went back to the room I would share with the old woman. She was watching television, in bed, in semi-darkness. My father picked up my suitcase. My mother wheeled me outdoors to the parking lot and helped me into the car.

I would rehabilitate at home.

My father carried my pop-up trundle bed downstairs to the living room, under a window that looked out onto our road. I was brought a small round table from the screen porch. My mother made sure there was always some food on it, usually a protein drink.

I staggered, with the help of a walker or a person or both, to the downstairs lavatory a few times a day. There was a toilet and a sink there.

For my evening trip, my mother brought three towels and a new white plastic chair into the tiny lavatory. I sat on the chair and gave myself a sponge bath.

A nurse came every other day to change the dressing on my central line. My physical therapist came three times a week. I remember the day I was able to walk up four steps. That happened in summer.

Once I was able to get myself all the way up the thirteen steps to the second floor of the house, I moved into my childhood bedroom.

I remember being strong enough to crawl upstairs but not strong enough to stand upright. I'd crawl to my bedroom, crawl up onto my bed, roll over onto my back, and slide down onto my feet. Ta-da!

My bath chair became my shower chair. I used my parents' bathroom, which had a shower stall.

I affixed my infant mobile, with its soft yellow and blue ducks, to my headboard once I was upstairs in bed, to celebrate the humiliation my life had turned to.

The Vascular Surgeon

The vascular surgeon always brought bad news: that I was going to have vascular surgery.

After the third time, after he recognized that I would brood and sometimes cry after he delivered his vascular news, he finished the consultation and walked out of my room.

The neurology team stood assembled outside the door, waiting to come in and practice examining me.

The interns and residents adored me. This was a small hospital, and a case like mine was extremely rare. Months later I'd learn that there were only six people on the entire East Coast with my disease who were available to take part in a drug study.

That day, after watching me weep a little, and after walking outside to find a cluster of residents and interns waiting for him to finish talking to me, the vascular surgeon said something to them.

He told them I was *the kind of patient who took things very hard*. My door was still open. He didn't care if I heard him say it.

He was about to do a third vascular surgery on me, and he knew I was twenty-one years old, and he knew that every time I recovered from a relapse of my disease, I was told I would stay well that time, and he knew I never stayed well.

And so the fourth time the vascular surgeon came into my room, expecting me to have remained the kind of patient who took things very hard, I had been practicing.

In my imagination I had been practicing the delivery of a line from a movie I loved. The line is spoken by a juvenile delinquent.

I had been practicing, and I didn't say a word while the vascular surgeon gave his usual speech. His central line speech.

I didn't say anything, and then he asked me if I had any questions, any concerns. He seemed to want me to continue to be the kind of patient who took things very hard.

But without even looking at him I said, *What can I say—I'm thrilled*.

He laughed like a high school kid, the way the science fair winner laughs when the guy with the police record insults the science teacher.

Vitamin K

After twenty-odd apheresis sessions, the veins in my arms had grown too scarred to access, and my body had grown too frail to tolerate having thick temporary catheters implanted in my chest and pulled after one week. I'd already had three of those.

And so it was time for a permanent central line.

But that would require a long surgery, with general anesthesia, which I wasn't in any shape for, so I couldn't get the permanent line right away.

I'd been taking azathioprine for two weeks, a cytotoxic chemo-therapy drug often used as an immunosuppressive. It had killed a lot of my red blood cells and a lot of my white blood cells. I was anemic and susceptible to infections. That was the cellular problem.

Then there was the plasma problem. Throwing away my plasma got rid of the devil antibodies, but my plasma also contained other cells and proteins that the blood needs. If they're missing, you get trouble.

My fibrinogens had disappeared almost completely. The hospital was doing a good job of removing my plasma and tossing out the fibrinogens with the bathwater.

Fibrinogens help knit the plasma together into a clot. When there aren't enough of them, you will bleed.

The evening before my surgery, my fibrinogen level was low. We'd been waiting for my fibrinogens to regenerate. But in order for that to happen, we had to take time off from replacing my plasma. So while the fibrinogens were coming back, the antibodies were coming back, too. So I was filling my blood with poison again, at the same time it was filling with the molecules I needed to tolerate the surgery.

My fibrinogen levels were checked all night, but by morning I still didn't have enough.

Two hours before I was to go in to surgery, an Irish doctor appeared. His brogue was beautiful and thick. He had been called to give me a shot of vitamin K, which would help my blood clot during the surgery.

He shot it into my right triceps. God, was he handsome.

The injection site stayed sore for five years, but not once during those years did I mind remembering the Irishman who had shot me full of K.

Juan

The morning of my fourth vascular surgery, I was awakened earlier than usual.

A new man entered my room. This is what he said to me, very slowly:

Hello. My name is Juan. One of my jobs. Is to deliver patients. To the operating room for surgery. Are you ready.

He looked at me and I saw that he believed his job, my life, and our time together were important.

And so looking back at him I said, *I'm ready.*

He reminded me to remove any jewelry or watches, and he took my watch off my wrist because my hands were paralyzed and I hadn't remembered to ask a nurse to do it for me the night before.

And then he transferred me from my hospital bed onto a gurney and wheeled the gurney out of my room, down the hall, into the elevator, out of the elevator, and into the presurgical ward, and then disappeared, without saying a word and standing up very straight the whole time.

Fear and Fright

I woke from the long surgery and saw my double-lumen permanent line and felt frightened. It looked like something I should pull out—a white dart, a poison arrow—but I couldn't pull it out. It was sealed under a clear plastic patch.

For the first day, doctors monitored the site through the patch, which covered part of my chest and my right side. The wound was fresh, and despite the pressure from the patch, the wound oozed.

The patch kept the ooze contained.

I had read Freud in school. He distinguishes *fear*, a state of worrying anticipation in relation to a definite object, from *fright*, the momentary response of our mind to a danger that has caught us by surprise but is already over.

And so when I looked at the plastic patch, I knew that what I was feeling, clinically speaking, was fright.

But the feeling didn't subside. Its sharpness lasted. So I looked down a second time, thinking the sight would no longer be frightening.

It was. And for hours I lay there, weeping in fright. Not fear. Fright.

The night nurse came in every couple of hours. After the second or third visit, when I was still crying from fright, she scolded me. But I wasn't sad. I was scared out of my mind.

So she gave me a tranquilizer.

I became addicted to them immediately and took one every night for weeks, and it wasn't long before I started needing more of them than the nurses wanted to give me.

Color

After I left the hospital with my permanent line, a nurse visited me at my parents' house every two days.

She (or, rarely, he) made a sterile field on the table next to me and peeled the seal of the patch covering the dressing on the entry site, and lifted the dressing. On the first day I said *it itches* and the nurse asked where and I said I didn't know because I wouldn't look at it with the bandage off. There were eight shallow stitch wounds below the big wound, in-and-out times four, but I didn't know that yet, and I could not touch the itch or point to it as it was in a sterile field, but the nurse hit the itch with a swab on the first try, and when I cried in relief she kept hitting it and I kept crying.

The stitches lasted eleven and a half months, which was as long as they needed to last before the line was removed.

This line was a Hickman line—the catheter entered the target vein but was first tunneled under the skin for a few inches, so the open wound was only a skin wound. This reduced the risk of infection. The hole in the vein was protected by my skin.

Every two days the visiting nurse flushed the line and dressed the wound and filled out a one-page summary form.

One of the categories in the summary was *Color*. For a while I didn't look at the copy of the form the nurse left in the white loose-leaf binder that had been provided by the home nursing organization. But then I did and saw that for the first two weeks I'd been home, the nurse had written the word *pale* on the line next to the word *Color*.

The next time she came, I protested when I saw her write the word *pale*. But she wouldn't change it.

The next time she came—she didn't come again. It was a new nurse, Fran. I told her, as she began to fill out the form, that the other nurse had written that I was pale, but that I'd always been pale, and that I wasn't anemic, and I was already taking so much iron I was almost completely unable to have bowel movements, even when I chased the iron pills with a double dose of stool softener.

Fran listened to me and wrote *patient is naturally pale* on the line next to *Color* and filed a copy of the form behind the ones the other nurse had left, and every time after that, she just put a check mark in the *Color* box to denote that my color was fine.

Fran was my favorite.

The Chair

On June 9, 1995, my mother helped me onto my father's antique wooden desk chair and pushed me to the bathroom.

I was a dead weight in the heavy chair. My mother, bigger and taller than I am, pushed as hard as she could. The chair's casters caught in our beige wall-to-wall carpet. Push, back up a few inches, rest. Push, back up, rest. When it was time to get up and onto the toilet, my mother held my upper arms very tightly, then lowered me down.

By afternoon my legs were completely paralyzed. My breathing had started to go. My mother phoned my neurologist and told him I was doing worse.

It was a bump in the road, he said. He believed my immune system would burn itself out, that it would stop producing antibodies and that I'd start to heal. It might happen today, even.

Then my mother phoned my hematologist.

The hematologist said we should hang up and call 911.

I heard sirens. An ambulance arrived, and a fire truck, and two police cruisers.

My mother answered the door and led the trauma guys upstairs, where I lay on the bed, still but able to chat. *I can't move my legs*, I told them.

The trauma guys, those Norse gods, strapped me into a fire-rescue chair, carried me down the thirteen steps to the first floor, lay me on a gurney, and rolled me into the back of the ambulance.

It was so green outside! Massachusetts was a green jungle. I could smell the trees.

Since it was rush hour, the driver turned on the siren.

Oldies

I wrote this three months after the diagnosis:

> *I listen to Oldies 103 now because if I listen to other people's music then my life won't really be mine. All day I hear songs about girls dying in car crashes and their boyfriends having to be good so they can see them again in heaven.*

> *If I get better, I know my life will be the same as it was before, and I already know it isn't worth suffering so much for. Not this much. And so I am trying to change.*

I started listening to Oldies 103 because it reminded me that something had happened to me while I was sick, and that I was different. And that even if I forgot to stay that way, I'd keep the habit of listening to the new radio station, and it might remind me.

I wrote this four months after the diagnosis:

> *I want to get better so I can be with the other people, the other dying people, who know the things they know.*

Other People

Most apheresis catheters like mine are implanted in women with breast cancer.

A visiting nurse asked me how long I'd had cancer. Then, after I told her I didn't have cancer, she swore, and apologized for swearing, and told me all the nurses in the office had gathered for a moment that morning in the break room and comforted one another that someone so young, so much younger than they were, was so sick.

Either before or after that—though it doesn't matter now, since I remember things in the order that they make sense— my primary care doctor visited me and said I'd already endured something much worse than most people have to endure in an entire regular-length life. His voice shook. He was forcing tears either forward or back.

Before the diagnosis, I would have loved hearing him say that.

The doctor was older than my parents, and he must have had plenty of younger patients, but he didn't understand yet that suffering, however much and whatever type, shrinks or swells to fit the size and shape of a life.

I refused to let him in my hospital room again, and my parents and I re-enrolled in our health plan with a different doctor. I felt no antipathy, just a certainty that his pity would accrue to me, and would grow in me like the sea of antibodies with which I was already invisibly killing myself, and that I couldn't take in any additional poison.

The Old Neurologist

During the first hospitalization, I'd been wheeled straight from Emergency to Radiology for a chest X-ray to ensure I hadn't aspirated anything, given my weak breathing muscles.

While she positioned the machine above my chest, the technician had asked me what was wrong with me. I must have looked healthy, lying there on the table. Nothing had atrophied yet.

I couldn't remember what they'd told me a minute or two earlier. I said, *It's something with BAR in it. Epstein-Barr?* I'd heard of that.

The technician paused. *Are you tired?* she asked. I wasn't tired. I told her I'd been having trouble walking and breathing.

Oh, Guillain-Barré! she said right away.

That wasn't what I had, either, but it was my official diagnosis at that point.

And it was what my neurologist called my disease when he saw me two weeks after I was released from my first hospitalization.

I went to see him because I'd developed the same symptoms as I'd had before my seven plasma replacement sessions, and the symptoms seemed to be worsening. My walking looked feebler.

It was hard not to monitor my strength obsessively. I'd check the rigidity of my fingers, spreading them out wide and straight, squeezing them with the fingers of my other hand. Then I'd do it again, two minutes later. And again.

And I'd get up and walk, and try to evaluate my gait. See if I could stand on my toes, on my heels. See if I could balance on one leg. Ask my parents to check everything and judge whether I'd grown feebler in the past four hours. Sometimes it was easy to judge, sometimes not.

My neurologist felt the strength of my large muscle groups, and measured my grip strength in both hands, and said the following sentence: *It's just a bump in the road.*

He knew that myelin grows back in patches, and that sometimes, while growing back, the patchy myelin can cause symptoms that mimic the pathology of myelin being stripped from the neurons.

And so he interpreted my symptoms as a bump in the metaphorical road toward wellness.

Three days later, when I was about to stop breathing, my parents took me back to the ER, where my lungs' vital capacity was measured, and within the hour I was back in Intensive Care having my plasma replaced.

After this sequence of events took place twice more, and I was sitting in my neurologist's office with symptoms I knew were worse than they'd been the day before, and which I knew beyond reasonable doubt were the beginning of another relapse, and after he said *bump in the road* again, looking cheerful and bored, I knew I was in trouble.

My neurologist never gave up trying to convince me that my relapses were bumps in the road. I was secreting antibodies as fast as the hospital could clean them out of my blood, and if I went eleven days without having my blood cleaned, my peripheral neurons would start sustaining major damage.

I already hated my neurologist by then. Every time I'd seen him after a hospitalization, he told me to pack my things and go back to college because the disease was gone.

Despite witnessing my first four relapses, my neurologist seemed to believe that plasma replacement would make my disease go away.

I could stagger to the bathroom twice a day with a walker and with one of my parents holding me partway upright. That, apparently, was good enough.

I think it was because he was tired of being told by a twenty-one-year-old girl that he was wrong that my neurologist recommended me to a doctor at another hospital.

The New Neurologist

After examining me and listening to me for less than five minutes, my new neurologist said I didn't have Guillain-Barré syndrome but a rarer, chronic form of the disease, called *chronic idiopathic demyelinating polyradiculoneuropathy*. He was right.

He recited a list of the treatments I'd have instead of apheresis, in chronological order of necessity. *If steroids don't work*, he said, *we'll try gamma, and then we'll try interferon, and since azathioprine didn't work, we'll try cyclosporine, and if that doesn't work, we'll try cyclophosphamide, and if that doesn't work, there are lots more drugs we can blast your immune system with.*

He said some of the drugs had bad side effects, but that a twenty-one-year-old person could handle a few side effects, and that a twenty-one-year-old person should not waste time with any treatments but the most aggressive.

He didn't approve of plasma exchange, which just tidied up the immune system's spill of poison into the blood without stopping up the leak that caused the spill.

He was like a Black Panther of pharmacology. *By any means necessary.* I loved him immediately.

I never saw my old neurologist again, and in a few years I heard that his partner, who'd covered my case for him sometimes, had lost his license after being convicted of having had sexual relations with a number of his elderly patients. Their practice was shut down, and I don't know whether my old neurologist moved to another hospital or quit practicing entirely.

Steroids

It's hard not to speak in clichés about corticosteroids.

They are powerful and make you feel better than it is possible to feel without them, and the more of them you take, the better you feel.

They are poison if you take them at a high dose for too long, and too long is generally considered more than six weeks. I took them for four and a half years.

In August 1995, when I couldn't stand up, I sat in a wheelchair in my new neurologist's office as he wrote me my first prescription for steroids, and I took 60 mg of prednisone the next morning, and 60 mg the morning after that, and that was the morning I got up and walked all the way from one end of my parents' house to the other and never needed a walker again.

I was finally able to eat a whole meal and no longer needed to drink two protein drinks per day. Not only that, but my parents and I were able to go out to restaurants, and I could walk to the table using just a cane.

And every meal, no matter how simple or cheap, tasted better than any other meal I'd ever eaten, and every piece of music I heard was more beautiful than any other piece of music I'd ever heard. This sounds like trite shorthand, but it is not.

I remember feeling well after having begun to take steroids, and how happy my mother was to cook a hamburger for me. I remember eating it. The ketchup, the mustard—I can taste the condiments.

I'm not talking about the way ketchup and mustard taste in general. I mean I can taste the particular condiments that were on that particular hamburger I ate in 1995.

I started staying up until four in the morning with a pile of books and magazines, and sleeping until seven, when I'd climb downstairs and make myself breakfast.

Sometimes I woke up screaming. Or, to be more precise, I'd waken from a dream of being in a death camp or a bad fire, so frightened that when I opened my eyes, I thought screaming might distract me from my fright. So I was always wide awake before I screamed.

And since my diaphragm muscles were quite strong by then, I could scream loud enough to wake my parents.

My father sometimes came to see if I were all right, if I had torn out my catheter as I'd slept, but only one of the stitches ever got torn out.

The catheter never got torn out in my sleep because I'd learned how to roll over slowly, even in deep sleep, while cradling the catheter in my left hand.

And I rolled over like that for a long time after the tube was pulled.

The Sixth Sense

The sixth sense is not psychic vision but proprioception, the perception of where the body is in space.

In October, during the first year of the disease, having already lost sensation, movement, and all my reflexes, I lost my sense of proprioception. Every night before sleep, my mattress folded into undulating spiral shapes and I stuck to the walls and somehow my head got to be five feet higher or lower than the rest of my twisted body. As long as it was dark, I stayed lost in imaginary space.

And so in October my neurologist added a proprioception test to my regular neurological exam.

This is what the book tells you: you have the patient close his eyes, and then you grab one of the patient's big toes and bend it either up or down, and you ask the patient whether the toe has been moved up or down.

But the book doesn't explain that the test is easy to cheat on. All you need to do is to feel the pressure on the big toe from the tester's hand, and if the pressure's on the top of the toe, then the toe's been moved down, and vice versa.

So I told my neurologist that the test was useless, and that in a properly administered proprioceptive sense exam, the pressure on the top and the bottom of the toe must stay equal and consistent throughout, so there won't be any clues from which to cheat.

After my neurologist learned that, the test was more fun, because I never knew how I'd do.

Hobbies

Six months after the diagnosis, I decided that if I had enough hobbies, it wouldn't matter if I stayed sick.

She's sick, I imagined people would say, *but she has so many hobbies.*

My father drove me to a nursery where I bought a bonsai tree, and I took all the books on bonsai out of the local library and filled a notebook full of notes.

I found the book of chess openings my famous chess-playing great-uncle had given me years before, and started memorizing. The Ruy Lopez opening. The English opening—my favorite one because it has only two moves.

The bonsai tree got uglier and barer and browner, and I let it die.

I remember thinking at some point that I'd already taken on hobbies beginning with *A*, *B*, and *C*, and how I'd eventually have one hobby for every letter of the alphabet, and then I would be busy.

I remember bonsai and chess, but I don't remember what the hobby that started with *A* was.

Hobbies grow exhausting, it turns out, just like any other obligation.

I was at a restaurant years later with a famous writer just back from the airport. On the plane he'd sat next to a woman who'd asked him what his job was, and he'd said *I'm a writer*, and the woman had waited a few moments and then asked him what his hobbies were.

I don't know what the famous writer said to the woman, but at the restaurant, he just said *Hobbies, can you believe it? I'm a* writer. *I don't have* hobbies. *My hobby is* writing.

My mornings were occupied by bathing, eating, drinking a protein drink, having my central line dressed and flushed by the visiting nurse, and exercising pathetically little with the visiting physical therapist. After the fourth or fifth hospitalization, I remember just lying in bed for hours every afternoon. I had too much to think about to do anything else. It must have looked as if I weren't doing anything, but I was very busy.

After I'd spent a few afternoons lying in bed looking as if I weren't doing anything, my mother and father came into my room with a small box wrapped in plastic. It was a computer program. *Chessmaster* 3000. My parents didn't buy me surprise gifts often. And so instead of gratitude I felt panic.

My parents must really think I'm going to die, I thought.

A Gift

Very late one night, in the fall of my eleventh-grade year, five years before the diagnosis, I unlocked the front door of my parents' house and went inside and closed the door quietly and locked it behind me, and turned on the hall light and tip-toed up the thirteen steps, and turned off the hall light, and felt my way along the railing that surrounded the stairs, and walked through the dark doorway of my room, and felt in the dark above my shoulder, to the right of the doorway, for the antique light fixture that had been installed in the 1920s when the house was built, and turned the small switch that felt like the head of a small smooth screw.

And hanging from the gooseneck of the light fixture was a dress hanger, and on that hanger was a black velvet cocktail dress with a V-neck and black velvet straps. And on that dress, just below the point of the V, my mother had fastened her rhinestone turtle pin, and I would wear that dress to the Wellesley Cotillion.

I put it on and it fit.

I made an appointment to have my hair French-braided at the salon downtown. My mother bought me a pair of black pumps with a small heel.

The Wellesley Cotillion took place every December at Wellesley College, and all the eleventh and twelfth graders whose parents lived in Wellesley were invited.

I say "whose parents lived in Wellesley" because the cotillion was a mixer for private school students who attended New England's various prestigious boarding schools. Most of the town's high-school-age students attended those schools.

The dance was first held in the 1940s, and it was called the Christmas Cotillion, and the public was not invited. It was very exclusive. You had to attend a certain very proper dancing school, which had admission requirements of its own.

In the late 1950s, public school students were invited for the first time.

None of us from public school in 1990 had been to a cotillion or attended an event that required formal dress—the freshmen and sophomores had only an informal dance, and the junior prom wasn't until spring. None of us had yet faced a receiving line.

In November the juniors at Wellesley High attended a special assembly where we were taught proper comportment at the cotillion. We were told to shake the hand of each man and woman on the receiving line, to make eye contact, and to state our names clearly.

There I am, about to face the receiving line, about to walk across the stage of my life in my town in my velvet dress. About to start learning why I don't belong here, why I don't want to belong here, yet do belong, whether I want to or not, in the torrent of people who walk through history in one direction.

The New Medicine

The first controlled study I took part in tested the efficacy of injected alpha interferon, an approved treatment for leukemia.

It was first-round research. And so everyone in the study—there were six of us—got the drug. There were no placebos.

I was excited about injecting myself with it.

I was excited until I learned that it was just a subcutaneous shot, not an intravenous one.

Years earlier, a doctor had told me a story about his internship at Bellevue Hospital in New York in the 1960s. During his rotation in Emergency, he was unable to find venal access in a patient whose arm veins were scarred from shooting heroin. So the patient said, *Why don't I just do it*, and took the needle, and hit a vein on the first try.

For this drug trial, I was given several little vials of interferon and a handful of syringes tipped with very small needles. Maybe an inch long.

Three times a week for six weeks, I sterilized the top of one of the vials with an alcohol swab, drew 300 cc of the serum into one of the syringes, flicked the syringe to get the bubbles out, wiped down a spot on one of my thighs with another alcohol swab, grabbed the flesh on both sides of the spot and pinched it with my left hand, then with my right hand put the needle in as far as it could go. Then I pushed the plunger all the way down, waited a moment, withdrew the needle slowly, and discarded it in my big red SHARPS container. The whole thing took less than a minute. It wasn't nearly dramatic enough that I could enjoy it.

On top of that, the side effects from the drug were the third worst of all the drugs I'd been given.

Interferon's main side effect is described as *flulike symptoms*.

I remember my father standing in the doorway of my room as I shook with fever in my bed. He looked a way I'd never seen him look before.

I wrote this in my journal on October 3, 1995:

> *My father cannot look at me, and when he finally speaks to me, he does so as though he is speaking to someone on the verge of death—that is, on the verge of death, and we're in a really bad play.*

Each time I gave myself my shot, I wanted to do it in front of someone. Did I want parental approval, encouragement that even though the injections were easy, I was doing something hard?

I walked into my parents' bedroom on those shot nights, carrying my works, and if my father was there, he'd get the look and leave. My mother stayed to watch the shot.

Twelve hours after my first injection, I was able to get out of bed. The worst of the fever was over.

But for six weeks I had what seemed to be a bad cold and cough, and a slight fever, and the medicine didn't do anything to help me stop secreting the antibodies, so I had to have apheresis all through the interferon treatment anyway.

And my data were removed from the study since so much of the drug had been thrown away with my plasma. On paper I hadn't been on the drug at all.

Certainty

One day my neurologist declared I was of nearly normal strength and that my exercise regime, three slow thirty-minute walks per week, was far in excess of that of the general population.

I must have looked puzzled, because then he said, *But you aren't playing tennis or doing anything fun.*

I wasn't. I didn't know when I'd lose all feeling in my hands and feet again, or need to save my strength for twice-daily trips to the bathroom, so it was hard to commit to a game of tennis, or even to a picnic, or a game of checkers.

I had moderate sensory deficit in my hands and severe sensory deficit in my feet. My hands and feet tingled and burned with fatigue and when I first woke, and there were numb patches on my shoulder blades and on my right calf.

I was still withdrawn from school and living with my parents, but my baseline strength was high enough that I could take a job at the bookstore where I'd worked in high school.

After a couple of weeks I had to quit so I could go to the hospital for a few days. The bookstore manager said I could have the job back when I was well again.

That happened twice, and the second time, the manager seemed to smile harder, to declare more vehemently that my job would wait for me. Maybe she feared I would sue her if she suggested my disability prevented me from doing the job.

It did, though. She'd already excused me from shelving new books. My arms weren't strong enough to lift a stack of hardcovers, and my hands weren't strong enough to wedge paperbacks onto the already full shelves. So I helped customers and punched sales into the register with my frail fingers.

After having to quit for the third time, I told the manager I wouldn't be coming back. I felt sorry for her. She had a kid by a man who had left her. She was angry except when singing along to "You're So Vain," which is what we played every night at nine-fifteen, after the doors were locked and we were counting the cash in the drawers and calculating the X-totals and Z-totals at the front and back registers.

My college boyfriend called the day before his graduation. I said hello, and then I said I didn't want to see him or speak with him. I already felt the numbness creeping into my hands, my face, my tongue. The antibodies would stay there until I replaced my plasma or died. *Sever all complications now*, the numbness said, *no matter how dear.*

The worst hour was the hour between the moment of deciding I should be taken to Emergency and the moment I got in the car.

I used that hour to call the bookstore manager, my thesis adviser, my physical therapist, the home nursing coordinator, and anyone else I'd made plans with before admitting to myself I wasn't going to stay out of the hospital—not this time.

I could have gone to the hospital without making any phone calls—everyone would have understood—but I preferred pretending I had *chosen* to quit everything. Chosen to get sick again. That it was all part of my plan.

I lied into the telephone receiver as I sat in a wooden kitchen chair, my aluminum walker leaning on the table next to me.

I'd covered the plastic grips of the walker with bright green pressure gauze and, over the gauze, a thin stripe of black electrical tape. Racing stripes.

Attention

My three temporary central lines had been precarious and de-
pended on my staying in bed, supine, because if I moved too
much, they would fall out and I would bleed. They went in
pretty close to my heart, so I wouldn't bleed long.

After my permanent line was implanted, I could go to the hospital for treatments without having to stay the night.

Along with plasma replacement, I was now trying a treatment
that a new study had shown to be more effective: a massive infusion of gamma globulin, a molecular component of the immune system.

The study showed that gamma globulin seemed to make the
immune system stop forming rogue antibodies.

Each of my gamma infusions was less than a quart of liquid,
but the infusion of that quart lasted from eight to twelve hours
because the human body cannot take concentrated infusions
of that particular protein any faster.

A liquid flowed from a machine into my heart. The mechanism was very simple.

After the first infusion, the insurance company sent the bill to my father by mistake. The infusion cost the insurance company thirty-five thousand dollars.

Eight or ten times during the infusion I walked myself carefully to the bathroom, dragging the machine and the bag and the tubing, the end of which was sewn to the outside of my body.

And I walked back again, to the blue reclining lounge chair in the small room.

Sometimes another person was there. We all wore appliances in our chests. The tubes were sewn to us and connected to the tubes of the machines that moved the liquids into us.

Before then, if I had to ride a train for half an hour or stand in a line at a shop for five minutes, I picked something up, or turned to someone, or ingested something, so the time would be filled with what I picked up or took in.

And also since then—but maybe not quite so much.

I say "the time would be filled," but the time was not so much filled as overfilled.

The time was already full before I put the new thing in. I overfilled my time, I think, to hide what was already there.

Some things are so horrible they need to be hidden right after they become visible. They are too horrible to be seen except very slowly, or in very small amounts. Or they are too beautiful.

There was a television set above my chair that received fifteen or twenty channels.

Here is a logical sequence of things to do in that small room. You arrive. You sit in the chair. You unbutton your shirt or take it off and put on a hospital gown that opens near your heart. You take the tubes in your hand and give them to the nurse. The nurse connects your tubes to the tubes of a machine that some fluid has been put into. The pump is turned on. You button your shirt around the tubes as best you can. You arrange yourself in a blue reclining chair. You press the button on the control that lights the television screen. You press it again until the screen changes to an agreeable picture. And you watch it. You get up and go to the toilet once every hour or two, pushing the pump on its casters. Once or twice, food arrives, and you eat. But mostly you read a book you have brought, or if you have not brought one, you watch the television, or you sleep.

After the first long infusion I felt different. Of course. The medicine was new. The experience was new. I was still in my first year of Latin, used to thinking hard before the meaning came. My parents came into the room to wheel me outside to their car and take me home. And they asked me what I had read and what I had watched on the television.

I had lain there in the reclining chair for ten hours, but I hadn't read anything or watched the television.

I was going to say *I had lain there for ten hours, waiting*. But I hadn't been waiting. I hadn't been anticipating the next moment. I think it was the first time in my life, which had lasted twenty-one years so far, that I hadn't done that.

I didn't know it at the time, but I was paying attention. I was not hoping I would learn how to do it, or despairing that I might not learn how to do it. I was unaware that I was learning or practicing or doing anything.

I was unaware I was doing anything except *nothing*.

Intimacy

One day in Oncology Outpatient, I sat with a woman who was having a bag of blood transfused. She beat me diseasewise—she had cancer—but I beat her linewise, because she had a slim little Hickman and I had my double-lumen monster.

She showed me her bald head under her brown wig and said she liked to shampoo the wig in the shower as if it were her hair.

Her husband had planned to buy her a mink coat on the occasion of their twenty-fifth wedding anniversary, but when she got cancer, she got the coat. She called it her *cancer coat*. It was dark and glossy, like her wig.

And she shared that she had lost her hair four times and been in many kinds of pain, but she agreed with me that the worst part about being sick was not having enough energy to feel powerful and fast. Not enough energy to run away.

After we'd been talking for an hour or two, the woman asked me what my name was. I was glad I hadn't suggested it first. We were ready to do it now.

Her name was Barbara.

Supplies

In December, eight months after the diagnosis, I decided I'd learn how to flush and dress my line. I still needed it. I was on my sixth month of periodic plasma exchange.

So I looked at the entry site with the bandage off, for just a moment, and that was enough progress for a few days.

But I got better at looking at the site, and my visiting nurse made me a booklet of three-by-five cards, tied together by a white string in the top left corner, that explained in steps how to flush and dress the catheter.

Even if I learned how to do it, my nurse would still have to visit me at school each week and look at the line, just to make sure nothing was wrong that I hadn't noticed.

I was as excited about learning how to care for my central line as my nurse was about visiting me at Harvard.

On my Nursing Visit Summary from December 21, 1995, Fran wrote:

*Pt uses excellent sterile technique for flushing line. She also
uses excellent technique for dsg Δ. Has some difficulties c̄
applying Tegaderm. Pt continues to feel stronger. One or two
more f/u + pt should be independent c̄ care. Next visit
12/23/95.*

On December 23, a different nurse wrote:

*This visit to f/u apheresis care. Pt performs flushing + dsg Δ s
error. She is very meticulous. Can be independent c̄ dsg Δ.*

I'd go back to school with enough medical supplies so I could
care for my line whenever I needed to. This is what I brought:

*1 large red biohazard container; 10 cc syringes; 5 cc syringes;
3 cc syringes; saline vials; heparin vials; vial spikes; needle
covers; interlink caps; injection caps; adhesive patches in three
sizes; gauze pads; nonsterile rubber gloves; individually wrapped
"sterile field" kits, each of which included 1 sterile waterproof
paper sheet, 1 pair sterile gloves, 1 sterile surgical mask, sterile
gauze patches, alcohol swabs, iodine swabs, adhesive compound
swabs, 1 roll sterile plastic surgical tape.*

I'd meet each week with my nurse and three times a month
with a representative from the company that delivered my
medical supplies and fetched my biohazard container when it
was full. It was a lot to do in addition to my treatment schedule and my classes, especially since I was feeble and couldn't
walk far.

Every couple of days I made a sterile field on my college desk
in Dunster J-22 and flushed and dressed my line. Once my

two suitemates, who are still my friends, sat on my bed and watched me do it. They watched and asked questions and listened.

I saved most of the flip-off caps from the vials of saline, heparin, and other solutions I infused. Each vial of solution was covered by a sterile bladder that could be pierced by a needle that drew the solution into a syringe. And each sterile bladder was covered securely with a plastic disc, its lip covering the lip of the vial, and each disc was stamped with raised letters that spelled FLIP OFF, because you were meant to press under the lip of the disc with the top of a thumbnail until the disc flipped off onto the floor or some other nonsterile area, so that nothing touched the vial's sterile bladder.

The FLIP OFF discs were chartreuse, pink, red, black, gray, white, or another color, depending on the solution in the vial.

I stuck the discs on my stereo and on every light switch in my suite. And I gave a lot of them to friends, who stuck them, with putty or with a small rolled-up piece of surgical tape, on their own light switches and on the switches of their electronic machines. Or in the middle of a wall.

I threw out at least a thousand discs. I wish I'd saved more of them. My old suitemates both still have a few.

Tableau Vivant

Tableaux vivants, living paintings, were planned for a winter gala at the Fogg Museum. I was part of a Monet painting and had to wear a pink gown with a plunging neckline. The tube showed. I pulled the bodice up. The top of the bandage still showed. A square of gauze and a frightening bump. I let it show. One girl saw it backstage and turned white and said my name as if she felt she had to.

The way someone says your name when you're making love and you know it's the only time you'll ever make love, and you aren't thinking about your partner's name, and you wish he hadn't said yours.

The Admiral's Nephew

Except for the very richest and a few others, Harvard upper-classmen live in one of twelve residential houses.

When a large group of homosexuals from my class were assigned to live in a historically preppy house, it was decided that the group would attend the notoriously conservative Eliot House Spring Fête in drag. A friend to the downtrodden, I had to find a tuxedo to wear.

Through a network of teenaged idealists, a tuxedo appeared. It belonged to a classmate whose family's roots predated the American Revolution and who had attended an excellent private school in New York.

The jacket was navy blue and double-breasted and had gold buttons, and it had belonged to my classmate's uncle, an admiral.

Though a few times that year I smoked marijuana with a clique of elite private school alums, in their dorm rooms that were nothing like mine—I remember a freestanding antique silver ashtray, and I remember some of the richest students had had their suite condemned for its filth—I knew our lives were already irreconcilable and that I would only ever be a tourist in theirs. And because I knew I was a tourist, I quietly gathered my small knowledge of the natives' ways and left scant trace of myself.

The lending of the tuxedo was a gesture of superb faith that we—the awake and living of the class of 1996, whether we had come from privilege or not—were, at least for a moment, of one voice. The lending of the tuxedo was a favor by a stranger, an intimate gesture made to benefit the general welfare of homosexuals.

Three years later, my suitemate, who had both kinds of friends, from both private and public schools, asked me whether I would be willing to help the admiral's nephew.

The nephew had enrolled in a video-making course, and his assignment was to make an edited movie of a process that involved the body. My suitemate had already watched me flush and dress my line by then, and she knew a picture of that would make a better movie than a picture of someone shaving his head, or putting on or removing clothing.

I don't like it when we refer to anything other than a corpse as *the body*.

But when my suitemate asked me if I would permit the admiral's nephew to videotape me flushing and dressing my line, I said yes.

While I had my central line I wore athletic bras because they were the only ones that didn't squeeze the wound site, and it was easy just to shrug out of one side of the bra before making the sterile field and changing the dressing.

I was less concerned that a handsome rich boy was going to see part of my right breast than I was ashamed he would see the hump of fat on my pimply shoulders and think I was a girl who not only had gone to public school but who had acne and was fat.

I wanted to tell him that the steroids had given me the acne. The steroids had made me fat. And the steroids had made me go to public school.

But in the end I just told him I had a rash on my shoulders and that it was from the medicine I had to take. He asked me if I'd like my face omitted from the final edit, and I said yes.

He gave me a copy of the tape but I've never watched it.

The Signet

After I began to understand the difference between public and private schools, and after I knew about the social register, and after I determined that class is determined not by schools or money but by family, and in spite of understanding that nothing I could do would ever deliver me from the middle class, I wanted to join the Signet Society, a social club for Harvard students that wasn't officially affiliated with Harvard and had a separate endowment and a private clubhouse.

It was a practice club for the exclusive Boston and New York social clubs the men and some of the women would join after graduation.

I came from a public school with GED tutors and auto shop, but I was elected to the Signet Society, and for my initiation, instead of shimmying up the pillar drunk while the officers held it at its wooden base, they laid the pillar on the ground and I stepped over it with my cane.

I wore a lavender gown and a twenty-inch tube that never clogged as long as blood thinner was shot into it every two days. From one direction it went into my right breast, under the collarbone and straight up, just under the skin, then into my jugular, so that halfway up my neck you couldn't see the shape of it anymore, and then it went into my subclavian vein and reached toward my heart. On the outside it hung like two white drinking straws, six inches long, with one red clamp and one blue one, like a piece of jewelry, and it was nothing like the expensive pendants the other Signet girls wore.

All spring I sat in my wooden chair like the others, and when it was my turn to ladle the soup at lunch I stood up proudly on my legs and did it. One girl wore a gold pendant shaped like a whale's tail. Her parents kept a summer house on Nantucket. I was proud to be as good as she was.

I already knew I could syringe the blood out of the tube in my chest and pick off the scabs where the tube went into me, and lie still while the doctors took fluid from my spine, or pierced my muscles with electrodes and turned on the juice, and for a long time I would not admit those things had been anything but an interruption in what seemed my life's larger project, which was to infiltrate the upper class and to be as good as those rich girls, and not once in the next ten years did I consider that the project of my life was not to wonder that I could pick up a ladle at that exclusive table, but that I could pick up a ladle at all.

More Medicine

Before the diagnosis I had had intercourse with only one person, the man I call *my college boyfriend*. Which sounds as if we loved each other all through college, but we didn't. We slept together for eleven weeks, and then he broke up with me.

I was very sad, but I enrolled in five classes the next semester and made a list of goals including *run at least twice a week* and *avoid all time-wasting social engagements*.

Two months into the semester, I got sick. And for a long time, I regretted I might die having had intercourse with only one person.

Like many freethinking college students, I thought intercourse was the greatest thing in life. And it just about killed me to hear of everyone's rambunctious affairs while I was in the hospital.

So when a medical student came into my room alone, after his rounds were over, with a book to lend or a mix tape he'd recorded, I thought about which medical students I'd invite to have intercourse with me if I got to the end of the road there, in the hospital.

But I went back to college still sick, with my central line, not having had intercourse with any medical students, and every month or so I went back to the hospital to sit in the Oncology Outpatient ward to have my plasma replaced or to have a bag of gamma infused. And the only people there were the hem-onc nurses, who were women.

My line was implanted in June 1995, and in May 1996, after eleven and a half months, it was pulled.

I wasn't well yet—I was taking steroids and gamma globulin. But those treatments kept me healthier than plasma replacement had. Those treatments actually slowed down the rate at which my immune system secreted the poisonous antibodies.

I would still relapse, but it was clear that the steroids and the gamma would keep me at least as well as apheresis would, so it was decided I wouldn't have my plasma replaced again. The gamma from March had already lasted three months. My neurologist believed I'd turned a corner.

I believed, though, that I would stop secreting antibodies forever only after I had intercourse. And though I looked worse than I ever had in my life—thanks to the steroids I was fat and swollen, covered in acne, and had a gruesomely round face— I knew I would have to go through the humiliation of finding a man who would agree to have intercourse with me.

I thought my friend Victor, who was legendarily promiscuous and who had shown interest in me shortly after my college boyfriend dumped me, might still be interested.

So I called him and invited him to have a drink with me that night. We had our drink and walked back to our dorm and sat down in the courtyard, just talking.

It was two days before Commencement. Early June. He was graduating, and I was graduating, too, sort of, but the envelope I was getting wouldn't have a diploma in it. It would be empty, because I had another semester of classwork to complete.

Since it was two days before Commencement, only the seniors were left at school, and everyone was awake, and most of them were in the courtyard with us. It was a party that had been going on all week.

And so I felt exposed—I felt too shy to seduce Victor in front of the entire senior class of Dunster House, even though I knew no one would notice or care.

Finally, Victor said, *Your place?* getting up from the bench we'd been sitting on.

And we went to my dorm room, which was a single suite I had all to myself, with my own living room and my own bathroom, because my neurologist had written a note to the university explaining I needed my space.

And we sat on my futon, taking turns drinking out of a plastic bottle of cheap vodka.

I was still unable to put the plan into motion.

Eventually Victor said, *Do you have any other rooms in this place?* and walked me to the bedroom, and lay me on my bed, and had intercourse with me.

Then he asked me about the scabs on my chest from where the line had just been pulled out of me, and listened to the things I told him, and held me very tightly.

Two mornings later, when we were in the courtyard again, seated in rows, about to receive our diplomas, he was wearing a buttoned shirt and sweating, because his neck was covered with bright red marks.

Almost seven years passed. Victor and I wrote every day. I lived in New York and he lived in Chicago.

He told me some of his secrets, and I told him some of mine.

Our letters were intimate, but I didn't get around to explaining to him that I'd recovered from my disease only because he had selflessly had intercourse with an ugly version of a girl he'd once had a crush on.

A little less than seven years after I was cured of my disease through the mystical power of intercourse, Victor had an aneurysm and died.

Cured

I remember three things about the gamma globulin infusions.

The first is that when I was in Emergency for the fourth or fifth time, and my breathing had become shallow enough for Triage Level 1, and I needed another central line implanted right then, I begged for gamma instead of apheresis.

But my blood was already too poisonous to leave as it was, and the doctors said they had to replace my plasma in order to remove the antibodies that were there already, or I might stop breathing.

So even though I was sobbing and begging not to be implanted with another line, I knew it would be implanted. I was too agitated to have the surgery right at that moment, so it was decided I'd be given a half milligram of lorazepam, which is what I was given when I had a panic attack.

Because of an administrative error, I was given four times the amount of lorazepam I was usually given. And I knew it. They gave me four pills instead of the usual one, and I didn't say anything. I was hoping I would pass out, but I didn't. Not quite. I was sedated just enough. The regular dose wouldn't have worked.

The second thing I remember about gamma is that during a later hospitalization, I was hooked up to a small pump, much smaller than the almost car-sized machine used for plasma exchange. At last we would see whether gamma would work.

It didn't do a thing except slur my speech for a few hours. And so for months afterward I continued with my tedious rounds of plasma replacement to clean up the poison that I still, despite the gamma infusion, continued to secrete into my blood.

And the third thing is that in March 1996, I had another infusion, of a much higher concentration than the first two, and received the infusion while lying in a meditative state in the Outpatient Oncology ward, and felt fine, maybe a little tired, and was driven home, and by the time I got into bed my head hurt so much I vomited. And I was sick for the next couple of days, too sick to think about the gamma.

But after that week was over, the tingling and numbness in my limbs wasn't any worse than it had been before the infusion, because the gamma had worked. Sort of. It didn't cure me, but I didn't relapse for four months.

The way I see it, gamma gave me three months, and Victor gave me one more after that and then some.

I didn't tell my doctors about Victor.

The Dump

After my third gamma infusion, my mother and I drove to the town dump on a weekday. Our town dump was not so much a dump as a futuristic recycling station with three kinds of glass, six kinds of plastic, two kinds of paper, compost and mulch and firewood, a book swap, and a section labeled *Recycle*, which was where you could get a pretty good pair of skis and where my parents got most of the furniture on the first floor of our house, including an antique Shaker chair.

My mother and I brought three of my canes there, and two walkers, including the one with the racing stripes.

And that day we ran into a neighbor, which was not uncommon. People went to the dump weekly, at least, to take a treasure hunt through Recycle. There were stage lights there that day, and I wanted to bring them home. Maybe because they were the heaviest things I saw there, and I wanted to see if I could lift them.

Our neighbor told us her mother had died just that week and that she was at the dump with some of the things from her mother's apartment. *Alzheimer's*, she whispered.

And my mother told our neighbor we were sorry, and that her mother, my grandmother, had had Alzheimer's, too.

Then the neighbor saw the pile of canes and walkers we'd just left on the ground, and looked at my mother, and indicated she understood how sad it was that my mother's mother had used those things until she couldn't walk anymore.

How sure our neighbor was that her suffering was the only kind of suffering.

And how sure I was that mine was worse.

1996

At some point after the year 2000, I read my journal from beginning to end and saw I had recorded nothing of consequence
in 1996 and threw away that year in disgust.

So I don't know what happened between my fake graduation
and my real graduation.

I remember feeling bereft that my class had graduated without
me. One of my suitemates moved to Romania, the other to
Borneo. Everyone's life seemed better than my life.

In the class picture, shot in June on the steps of Widener Library with a rolling camera, for which at least a thousand of us
were present, I stand between two handsome friends, one of
whom later worked as a catalog model. In the photo my face
is absolutely round. It is one of only a few photographs I allowed anyone to take of my steroid-poisoned body.

In the fall of 1996 I enrolled in my final semester of college.
I was in love with someone I'd met in New York and rode the
Greyhound bus from Boston to New York and back at odd

times. Once I took an early bus back from New York on a Tuesday morning and made it to my Tuesday afternoon poetry class on time.

After college I moved to New York and lived in the obligatory small apartments full of friends and friends of friends, knowing I'd be leaving in six months for graduate school. I had the usual adventures people have when they move to New York.

Calendars

My mother keeps her monthly desk calendars. They're compact: one month per page, one square per day, two inches by two inches. Once in the 1980s I saw her take down a few from the 1970s, from her closet shelf, and look through them.

I called her today, in 2006, to ask if she'd send me her calendars from 1995 and 1996, but she's thrown all the old calendars away. Last month she did it.

Why should I save them? I'm never going to be famous! she said.

Secrets

One day in 1997 I was at Mars Bar, on the Lower East Side, with the man I was having an affair with. The man had a girlfriend. We played chess at the Thompson Street chess store and went out to dinner and made out in cabs. I was twenty-three and had everything I wanted.

I was still taking steroids, but my excitement at having got well enough in two years to graduate college and move to New York had made me furiously happy.

I was an intern at a magazine, second shift, three or four nights a week. Afterward I'd go to Pravda with the man I was having an affair with, and we'd drink chocolate martinis, which were a fashionable drink that spring.

So one day we were at Mars Bar with a friend of the man I was having an affair with.

The friend seemed manic. He was funny and verbal. We all took turns telling our best drug stories.

Then the friend of the man I was having an affair with said, *The best drug I have ever taken was steroids.*

And I said, *Me too! Do you have MS?* I knew that multiple sclerosis and its sister diseases, like mine, were commonly treated with high-dose corticosteroids.

The bar was very loud. The man I was having an affair with didn't hear. By then a few more people we knew had shown up.

The friend of the man opened his eyes wide and said *No!* but didn't mean it. I took him aside and apologized, but I wasn't surprised when he began to weep. He said, *I've never been able to tell anybody that*, and I hugged him.

His tears seemed fake, though, and I wasn't surprised when he became an actor.

Iowa City

In August 1997 I moved to Iowa City to go to graduate school. I brought a letter from my hematologist noting the concentration and rate of the gamma globulin infusion I'd need if the disease relapsed again.

I loved Iowa City. It was small enough that I was able to know it thoroughly.

I didn't bring a car. I didn't like driving. I'd loved living in New York and walking everywhere.

And so even though Iowa City wasn't as pedestrian-convenient as New York, I walked everywhere.

I walked all the way up Gilbert Street to the Asian grocery store where I could get Korean noodle bowls. The kind I liked was called *I'm Hot*.

I liked cooking the oily noodles, draining them and mixing them with a can of tuna, then tossing everything with the contents of the spice packet and a couple of tablespoons of water.

I went to the Korean grocery every two weeks.

On maybe my fifth trip to the grocery, I noticed a small build-ing just past it, on Gilbert.

It was a plasma donation center!

The rates for plasma donation were posted in the window. I think it paid $45 per liter.

One day a woman in my graduate program told me that she donated plasma twice a month, which was as often as they'd allow it. And I remember how excited I felt, the moment be-fore I told her how much plasma I'd used, plasma that had been gathered at donation centers like the one on Gilbert.

Before and After

When I turned twenty-two I thought my life, which had already been relatively easy, would get even easier, since at twenty-one, I'd already done the hardest thing I'd ever have to do.

The only hard thing I'd ever done had not left me compassionate.

I remember the first friend I made who met me after the diagnosis, but I don't remember when I stopped thinking, when I met new people, *This person, whose hand I am shaking at this moment, is another person who never knew me before the diagnosis.*

The only hard thing I'd done in my life was recovering from a disease. My self-image had been highly susceptible to that event. It constituted most of my identity.

When a friend or a stranger mentioned anything about a difficult or noteworthy event, I chose one of countless hospital vignettes from recent memory and told the little story in a way that prevented further conversation about it or any other subject.

Though during the bad relapses I knew I was a better person temporarily, in general the disease made me furious, jealous, resentful, impatient, temperamental, spiteful. My sense of entitlement grew enormous. I knew the steroids had triggered what is now called a *mood disorder*, and I didn't care.

The hardest thing I'd ever done, the hardest thing I'd ever have to do, had made me a worse person! That wasn't how it was supposed to work. Tribulation is supposed to make strong people, people who radiate mercy, leaders of their kind.

I'd have to do harder things before my self-regard lost the mean air that had inflated it.

The Price

Prednisone's long-term side effects include depression and mania, weakness and fatigue, blurred vision, abdominal pain, infections, painful hips and shoulders, porous bones, acne, insomnia, weight gain, stretch marks, facial swelling, and nervousness. There are others. Those are just the ones I have.

Textbooks refer to the side effects as *premature aging of the body*.

The sore spots below my cheekbones make it hard to lie down without a soft pillow. I can't lie on my side on a flat surface. I lie on my belly and rest my skull on the tip of my nose and lift my head for periodic breaks.

When I hold a long melismatic vowel, my facial muscles tire. That is, if I sing *Ahhhh* for a few seconds, all the little muscles around my mouth start to twitch.

I gobble calcium supplements to keep my osteopenia from turning into osteoporosis, but someday it will. I'll break a hip and it won't heal, and I'll become bedridden and develop pneumonia and suffocate.

In San Francisco I met a man who was missing a big chunk of his jaw. The conversation turned to a certain type of hospital visitor. *Have you considered herbal remedies?* this visitor asks. Both the man and I had entertained this visitor.

Herbal remedies! They're less toxic to me and to the earth. If I don't live long enough to break a hip, it will be because I get cancer, an ironic side effect of Western cancer drugs.

Western medicine saved my ass, the man said. He wasn't smiling. That's all he or I needed to say.

Mary

Before there was much of an Internet, I wrote a letter to "Confidential Chat" in *The Boston Globe* saying I would appreciate hearing from others who had Guillain-Barré syndrome or who knew anything about it.

I received fifteen letters in response. Most were handwritten, and a few were typewritten, with plenty of whited-out errors.

A woman named Gayle wrote this to me:

> Prior to GBS I was into weightlifting and Truck Driving. I could lift well over 100 lbs. After GBS I couldn't lift a 2 lb sand bag, it was very discouraging at first but then I kind of got angry and started working really hard to get my self back to where I was prior well I am half the way on the weight lifting, and back to every activity I was in prior, I just don't have to much strength I get tired out alot quicker, sick alot quicker. It doesn't happen as quick as you'd like it to, but patients it will. I do remember the one thing that really got me frustrated though, it was the soda cans, I couldn't open them, for the longest time.

Besides the fifteen letters, I received a mesh rectangle of gray and white embroidery spelling the word *JESUS*.

In 1999 I found an online bulletin board for people with CIDP. Its posts described even the weirdest and rarest symptoms and side effects, and each post had drawn dozens of responses.

Plenty of adults wrote on the board about themselves or their children.

One poster asked whether there were any young adults on the board, people in their teens or twenties. The woman who'd written the post was named Mary, and she was from Dublin, Ireland, and she was twenty-one years old.

And I was twenty-five, and so I wrote back. We wrote to each other almost every day.

Mary wore metal braces on her legs and lived with her mother and saw her neurologist only once a month or so, and it was only then that she could have apheresis. That was the best her country's health-care system could do for her.

Mary and I exchanged photos many years later, after she'd moved to Spain and then to France, and had undergone apheresis in four countries, and after she'd taken the braces off her legs so she could try pressure stockings instead, and then put the braces back on after the stockings didn't work, and after she'd dated two Parisian men at once and done mountains of cocaine and got blind drunk in more countries than I have even visited, and I saw, without surprise, that she is an absolute knockout.

Soldiers

This is how I wound up in lockdown.

First I took prednisone for four years.

Then I had abdominal surgery. There was a tumor on my left ovary. Benign. Lemon sized. I was in the middle of my second year of graduate school, but I had to have it out. My lover and I found it in the usual way. He was lying down. I was sitting up. Then I felt a pain, and we had to stop. Later we found out he had moved my ovary.

So I had the surgery during the spring semester, and because I had been taking prednisone for four years I had to be given a bolus of the steroid to help my body through the surgery. The adrenal glands get lazy when there's already so much steroid in the body, and when it's time for the glands to produce a lot of adrenaline, suddenly, when the body is under great stress, stress like an abdominal surgery, the lazy adrenal glands are too sluggish to keep up with the body's demand.

This adrenal suppression occurs if prednisone is taken for longer than seven days.

Coming out of general anesthesia, I shook so horribly that I went to the ER to make sure I didn't have an infection. Prednisone weakens the body's ability to fight infections, and in the previous four years I'd had a lot of them—fungal, viral, bacterial. They were hard to treat. I always had at least a couple of rashes going.

I knew, though, that if I were shaking from a postsurgical blood infection, I could die pretty quickly.

In the ER I had no fever, but the doctors tested my blood pressure lying down, seated, and standing, and saw that my heart wasn't working very well, so they gave me another steroid bolus. It went in and in fifteen seconds I stopped shaking and felt wonderful. Euphoric. Which is normal after a shot like that.

Then my lover, who had moved my ovary, drove me home.

But in a couple of hours I started shaking again. My muscles were cramping, and the pain got so bad that we went back to the ER for another bolus.

Then the whole thing happened again. On the third ER check-in, I was admitted to the hospital.

We didn't know yet that it hadn't been a dearth of steroid that had caused the shaking but an overdose. And that after that overdose, of course, I had been given three more shots.

After the three shots, lying in my room at the hospital, I began to hallucinate. The condition is referred to as steroid-induced psychosis.

I saw soldiers in my room. They were dressed in red uniforms with tails and gold buttons. They were British soldiers from the American Revolution.

They were there, of course, to prevent their territory from being taken over from within. They were my blood, and the revolutionary soldiers, absent from this scene, were my antibodies.

The soldiers paced quickly around my bed, their swords by their sides, looking at the ground, but I could see their solemn faces, which showed me they would fight to keep me safe.

Despite my soldiers, I felt so agitated from the massive amount of extra steroid in my body that I was screaming. I screamed until I ran out of breath and then took breath to scream again. I got out of bed and ran in place like a boxer. I was running and screaming because I was full of adrenaline. My body had made a sensible decision.

A nurse heard me screaming and gave me a shot of Demerol to calm me down. I stopped screaming for half an hour. Then she gave me another shot of Demerol.

In a couple of hours I had been given as much Demerol as the hospital would give me, so I spent the rest of the night running in place and screaming. Since I was hoarse, the screaming was quiet.

Lockdown

The next day, I am told, I had several visits and phone conversations with people from my graduate program.

They called and visited because the director of the program had spoken with a representative from the hospital and misheard the phrase *adrenal failure* as the phrase *renal failure*. And she had announced to everyone that they should call or visit to say goodbye, because I would soon die.

I don't remember the visits or the phone calls. Later I heard I'd told a visitor that I'd slept with someone else from our graduate program, which I had, once, a year before.

In a few days I was discharged from the hospital and moved back into my apartment, but I hadn't recovered from the overdose.

In two months, unable to get out of bed, I called my parents in Massachusetts and said I needed them to come to Iowa and bring me home.

I had a fever, aches, rashes, muscle weakness, and extreme fatigue.

As soon as I was back in Boston I went to see my neurologist, expecting he'd send me right downstairs to be infused with gamma globulin.

But my neurologist said the weakness and fatigue weren't CIDP symptoms, and he was right.

He said there was nothing he could do to make the symptoms go away, and that it was a separate, probably viral, syndrome, and that I should see an infectious disease specialist.

I got home, got into bed, and began yelling with grief, which was something I hadn't done before. Again, as it had in the hospital in Iowa, my body decided sensibly on a course of action. I was too sad to cry. I had to yell. The yelling relieved my sadness better than crying would have.

After five more months of the fever and the other symptoms, the cause of which was never determined, and after living at my parents' house all that time, mostly in bed, I woke one day knowing I couldn't tolerate another day of my life, that this would be the last day. I told my mother. She asked me how I was going to do it, listened to the answer, took away my car keys, locked the garage, and drove me to see a therapist, who talked with us together, and then to my mother alone.

Then my mother drove me home and helped me pack a few things. And drove me to a different hospital from the one where I'd spent so much time being treated for CIDP.

During the evaluative interview, I made one mistake. I said I didn't believe I would ever get better from whatever was wrong with me.

And so I was admitted, with severe depression, to the locked ward.

I was still taking a daily dose of steroids.

Last Words

Wait—what would I have done if I'd been told one of my classmates would soon die of renal failure at twenty-five?

Would I have phoned? Visited? Brought a gift?

I was told that two men from my graduate program called me. One poet and one fiction writer. I don't remember.

It is sweet to imagine the conversation they might have had before calling me. One of them asking the other if he'd like to come over and talk with their classmate, together, before she died.

Maybe afterward they talked with each other about how I'd sounded—as if I would soon die, or as if maybe I wouldn't.

What would I have done? If it were, say, the guy from New Hampshire I'd always liked? I think I'd have called him.

What if it had been the girl with the glass eye, whose life seemed so boring, with her fiancé and her car and her many hobbies? I'd have sent a card, maybe.

The stunning woman from Brussels—she visited. And brought a pile of magazines. But now that I think of it, she may have sent the magazines with someone else. It is hard to remember. I was blacked out, so anything seems plausible.

I like to think I would have said something to the dying person.

Would I have written about the dying person?

If I were a little in love with the dying person, would I have written little secret poems about this love? Would I have showed them to anyone, submitted them for publication?

Did anyone do that?

How did my classmates experience my death by renal failure in 1999?

Prayer

Once in my life I promised to say a prayer for my Catholic grandmother.

I picked up the phone when she called one morning at seven o'clock. She begged me to come and visit her. She said she was lonely. She was eighty-three years old and her friends were dead. I said I would visit if I didn't have to go to school. I was in the seventh grade. She said, *Oh, school.* Then she thought for a moment and said, *Say a prayer for me.*

I was self-conscious generally, and prayer embarrassed me. I had learned phonetic Hebrew and had been taught Hebrew prayers, which, to me, were just a sequence of sounds, but I didn't know how to pray in English.

After my grandmother's death I remembered my promise and felt sad, but less about my grandmother than about the idea of a young person promising to say a prayer for an old person and then forgetting to do it during the old person's lifetime.

Twelve years later, in the psychiatric ward, I was eating crackers in the kitchen when two other patients sat down with me.

One woman was my age. She was schizophrenic and had spent her first few days in the dayroom, standing, holding a Bible, reading loudly and clearly, and sometimes singing in a pure soprano.

The nurses asked her to stop. Later she explained, *I just wanted to bring the Lord into this place.*

The other woman was poor and had a very ill son who lived in a state home. Like many of the patients, she chewed nicotine-laced gum, because smoking on the ward was prohibited. And like all of us, she had no pretensions of superiority to anyone else committed to the ward.

She asked me, *Do I seem depressed?* I looked at her desperate, ruined face, and answered with careful solemnity, *Maybe a little.*

The ward was the only true community of equals I have ever lived in. What I mean is that we all knew we had already lived through hell, that our lives were already over, and all we had was the final descent. The only thing to do on the way down was to radiate mercy.

The singing schizophrenic, the sad mother, and I sat quietly for a few minutes, and then the schizophrenic asked, *Would you like to pray with me?*

The two women and I joined hands. One of them spoke for a while and then stopped. Then the other spoke. They addressed God humbly and directly.

One said, *Please take care of my friends Nico and Sarah, and help us leave this place.*

Then she said, *I love you, Jesus.*

I hadn't ever heard my Catholic grandmother speak to her Lord like that. And the rabbi at my synagogue never seemed to want much to do with a heavenly God.

The schizophrenic was allowed to leave before I was. Her parents came to get her and seemed terribly ashamed. But to me she seemed no more or less joyful, no more or less insane, than on the day she'd arrived and first sung in the dayroom.

The only changes I noticed in her were what looked like painful muscle spasms from her antipsychotic medication, of which she now took a higher dose.

Kimiko

I awoke on my first Sunday on the psych ward to find a roommate. She was Japanese and she didn't speak. In one hand she held a slip of paper with some sentences printed on it in pencil. One of them, I read later, was *I understand I need to talk for discharge but I don't like to talk when I have pain in my heart.* She held up the paper while she sat in a chair, folded almost in half.

Her face and neck were blue.

What I mean is that she had come in during the night and found the whiteboard and the sweet-smelling blue marker we used to write down each other's phone messages, if anyone called, and if we could remember what to write, and if we remembered it's a good thing to be seen doing if we wanted outdoor privileges.

Kimiko found the marker and—I was not there, I am only filling in the narrative based on the part I could see—her desolation was so total that the only relief she saw was to scrub her face out with the blue marker. Her whole neck and most of her face: small blue vertical scrub marks.

The doctor was explaining that she had to wash it before she'd be allowed to participate in Group. I wondered what this doctor understood and hoped it was something, because I am not a doctor and I understood Kimiko needed to have a blue face.

Also she would not put on any clothes. The doctor seemed not to understand a person can be too sad to wear clothes. I asked the doctor to go away.

Kimiko wasn't allowed food unless she left our room, so she sat in the corner of the dayroom all day, naked and wrapped in a sheet, her blue face visible under her white hood.

My parents visited. That Sunday was the day of an important football game, and my father sat in the dayroom with the other mental patients and watched it. While he was there Ed the psychotic came out of his room in hospital pajamas and asked Betty, a near-catatonic depressive, what she was going to be for Halloween, since it was only a week away. Ed said, *I'm going as a mental patient.* He'd been on electroconvulsive therapy and Haldol since 1976.

On Monday Kimiko had ECT and on Tuesday declared she felt better. Her husband was a scientist in the States on a fellowship. I got her to teach me how to say *I am not insane* in Japanese: *wa-ta-shi-wa ku-ru-tte i-nai.*

Darlene and Sam

By Saturday, still on the psych ward, I could feel my hands were weaker, but Darlene said my walking looked the same, no worse.

Darlene was sixty, very skinny, a long-haul anorectic. Did jigsaw puzzles ten hours a day and was thoroughly sweet to everyone, even Betty, who dozed in the dayroom and smelled.

Sam the bulimic told me about Darlene's repeated suicide attempts—the eating disorders trusted each other. We both smiled. Darlene knew what she was doing.

That night we all stayed up playing poker with candy for chips. It was Edith's first game of poker. She was an old lady whose antique shop had burned down. I taught everyone Texas Hold 'Em. We'd all taken our meds before starting and had to quit after the fourth hand.

My second Sunday on the psych ward was Halloween. We decorated the ward with spiderweb floss. Sam had three trays of pastries sent from his shop. The therapist from South

Dakota danced a jig. Ed and Nico danced cheek to cheek. Darlene sang "Crocodile Rock." Edith recited a Yeats poem.

On Monday, in art therapy, I glazed my trivet, a square of plaster set in metal, with rows of tiny heart-shaped tiles set in the plaster.

More Cause and Effect

After four days on the ward, I was allowed to sign out for a chaperoned walk around the parking lot. Three days after that, I signed out on a day pass. My parents came to get me and drove me to the computer store because I believed every document on my hard drive would self-destruct on New Year's Day. I spent my day pass loading new software and manually re-opening and resaving each one of my files.

That night I went back to the ward feeling good about my successful day off from lockdown. I'd avoided unhealthy behavior, as long as I didn't count the obsessive reformatting of hundreds of digital text files. My success earned me the right to ask to be released.

I left the psych ward a few days after Halloween.

Instead of going home, though, I had to go to the other hospital, the one where I'd spent so much of the mid-1990s, because my severe depression, which I'd mistaken for a CIDP relapse, had triggered a CIDP relapse.

Uncertainty

In the twelve years since my diagnosis I have not owned a home or a car, or had any job that wasn't temporary, or married or lived with anyone.

I belong to an artists' union and pay for its group health plan with freelance money and with the money I inherited when my grandfather died.

I'm thirty-two years old and I'm an unwed, adjunct-teaching, freelancing renter. But New York is full of people like me. Everyone in the city I know who owns property or has kids has one of two things: a full-time job or rich parents.

There exist several rationalizations for my life. I'm holding out for a teaching job that suits me. My parents aren't rich. A full-time office job would sap my energy. I don't want to buy a place until I'm sure I won't meet someone who'll share the down payment with me. And each of these explanations is reasonable enough.

But I know the real explanation is that I haven't lost the fear that at any moment I will have to quit my job, say goodbye to my friends, leave my home, and go to the hospital not knowing when, or in what condition, I'll be discharged.

My disease has been in complete remission for seven years, but I still act as if I expect it to come back tomorrow.

Bones

In 1997 I stubbed my toe on the leg of a cast-iron chair and bandaged my purple foot and tore the insole out of a sneaker so I could fit my foot into it.

After watching me limp for a few days, my boss at the magazine made me go to a clinic, where they took an X-ray and announced I had three fractures.

In 2000, the first night I was back in New York after graduate school, I went to a roller-skating party at Chelsea Piers. I was curving left on my skates, at the narrow part of the oval rink, and lost my balance and fell backward. I caught myself on the heel of my right hand, and my arm hyperextended and my radius hit my humerus very hard and broke.

I'd felt the bone break, but just to be sure, I skated to a pay phone and called my friend's father in St. Louis. He was an army doctor. He asked me how my arm and hand felt when I moved it up, down, around, how my fingers felt. Then he said I should go to an ER and have an X-ray taken.

I thanked him and thought to myself, *Well, so I'll have a broken arm for a while.* I wasn't going to another ER ward ever again. Not if I were conscious.

Five days later, while trying to chop carrots with an arm I knew was broken, I called my friend Vivian and said I wouldn't be able to cook dinner after all. I had invited her over to prove my arm wasn't just functional—it was good enough to julienne carrots. I hailed a gypsy cab and told the driver to take me to the nearest hospital. I should have taken the subway to a good hospital on the Upper East Side, but I didn't know any better, so I wound up at Woodhull Medical Center.

In the Emergency waiting room were two men in orange jumpsuits, handcuffs, and leg irons, covered in blood, eyes swollen shut, and two or three police escorts for each of them.

A nurse asked me if I would please come into a ward to translate for a Polish patient, and I told her I didn't speak Polish, and she stared at me until I noticed I was the only white person in the waiting room. The only pale white people treated at Woodhull were Polish immigrants from Greenpoint.

A doctor took an X-ray and gave me a sling and told me to come back in a week. I didn't. The radial head fracture didn't heal properly, but I don't mind.

I've always had health insurance—if I relapsed without insurance, my parents would be homeless within a year—but other than that visit to Woodhull, I didn't see a doctor for two years after I got out of lockdown.

In 2004 I fell on my kneecap while chasing my friend's dogs in an ice storm in rural New Jersey. I drove myself to an orthopedist, skidding all the way, knowing I'd need surgery to fish out the bone chips. God, it would be horrible. I'd be admitted to the bone ward and everything would go back to the way it was when I was helpless.

But all the calcium supplements I'd taken, all the miles I'd run, had made my bones strong again, and I hadn't broken my kneecap.

Even now, when I crack a bone on something hard, I still think I've fractured it, and in a flash I can see my wasted body in a bed with side rails, but I haven't broken any bones since the night I broke my arm at Chelsea Piers.

Scars

For years I liked thinking of the ways I would erase all traces of the disease.

First I would stop taking the steroids.

Then I would have someone unclasp the impossible clasp of my MedicAlert bracelet.

Then I would go to physical therapy every day and my muscles would grow, and my heart and lungs would strengthen, and the fat deposits in my face and on my upper back would melt away, and I would run three miles along the Charles River, which was what I did at least twice a week during the month before the diagnosis.

I would apply expensive creams that would dry up the steroid acne.

I would have my teeth bleached of their tetracycline stains.

And so on.

Finally I would have plastic surgery for the thirty scars on my chest from the four central lines. I ruminated on that surgery obsessively. It was the last thing! The last thing, and then all evidence of the disease would be gone forever. No one, not even I, would be able to tell I'd been so sick.

I stared at the scars in mirrors. I could point to the four large ones without a mirror, without even looking down. I could practically feel them on me.

Once the disease went into its most recent remission, the one that's still going on, I got fit again, just as I'd planned.

In 1996, I'd given all of my scoop-necked tops to my roommate, as it would have been rude to walk around with a big wound and a couple of tubes flopping around, scaring everyone.

For years after the line was out, I didn't wear anything that exposed the scars.

But now that I look quite healthy, I like exposing them, and I don't want the plastic surgery anymore.

The Point and the Ray

I grew used to being sick and looking forward to recovering.

Then I grew used to being well again for a short while, know-ing I'd be sick again sooner or later.

Then I grew used to having no prognosis at all, because with a mysterious disease, all things are possible.

My existence shrank from an arrow of light pointing into the future forever to a speck of light that was the present moment. I got better at living in that point of light, making the world into that point. I paid close attention to it. I loved it very much.

And then one day, my life was a ray again, and the point was gone.

I tried to find that point after the latest, longest remission began.

I thought of the point as a moment in spacetime where I could be free of all memory and all desire—a point that existed apart from everything before and after it.

Sometimes I can feel myself getting close to finding the thing in spacetime I lost by getting well.

. . .

I didn't start writing this until my body made another decision.

The day before the decision I wrote, *Can't catch my breath all morning because of a wildness in my body that is like birds flying me toward his body.*

The next day I wrote, *I resisted as long as I could. A narrator must keep a safe distance from the story, but a lyric speaker must occupy the lyric moment as it's happening. Or so it seems to me at this moment.*

A crow stands outside my window all day, reminding me of the best thing about my life—that it ends.

I think my body's decision shone a light on the memory that once my body steered me. Or that it steers me.

Music

How long was I sick?

I know that March 26, 1995, was the morning I awoke with numb feet.

But before that morning, I'd had a head cold stirring in my body for weeks—an infection for which my immune system had been generating antibodies on top of antibodies.

That head cold triggered the mechanism in my immune system that resulted in the syndrome called CIDP.

But it wasn't the head cold—it was the great beauty of the Allegri piece that had made me keep the head cold in my body for so long. It was the promise of singing that Allegri solo that made me keep the virus from running its course. I had to put off the cough until after that performance, and instead of going away, the virus waited patiently to be allowed to make me cough.

But that story began in the seventeenth century, before Mozart was even born.

So when did I first get sick?

Getting sick was a process just as getting well was a process.

The most important things must happen slowly, incrementally. Just think—they are always painting some part of the Williamsburg Bridge! This is why moments of transformation are so exciting.

But what appeared as a transformative moment, the moment I awoke on a Sunday with numb feet, only *felt* like a transformative moment.

When

How long was I sick?

I got the tube pulled in May 1996. I recovered from my last acute CIDP relapse in November 1999. I recovered from my last severe depression in March 2004.

In May 2004, to treat my more or less constant steroid-induced hypomania, I stopped taking olanzapine, which I'd taken for five years, and began taking quetiapine fumarate.

And this may sound silly or arbitrary or vain, but after I traded olanzapine for quetiapine fumarate, I lost twenty-five pounds in six weeks. And those twenty-five pounds, which I'd been carrying since I'd first gone on steroids in 1995, was fat I couldn't burn off with exercise or by restricting my food intake. It was from the drugs.

Once that nine-year-old fat was gone, I looked healthy even to myself. I ran and ran. I got lean and strong.

I was thirty years old, and most of the women I knew were fatter and curvier than they'd been as college students, and I'd thought for the past nine years that that had happened to me. That I'd taken on the shape of the adult woman my genes had programmed me to become.

It was a joyful and confusing time, 2004. I'd become accustomed to being one shape, and suddenly I was a different shape.

My gait changed. I became lighter on my feet. I had to buy all new clothes.

I became furiously happy. I ran a lot and drank a lot.

In 2004 I ran three miles for the first time since college, and even though I am even now still taking quetiapine to treat the hypomania, I've integrated the drug's side effects into my life.

Also in 2004 I made a mistake in the midst of an unstable euphoria, and in 2005 I took my last drink. In penance.

And after the requisite horror of the first six weeks, the first six months, the first sober dates, the first sober sex, the first sober year, sobriety made me feel better than I'd ever felt.

I say 2004 is the year I got better, because it's the year the biggest problem in my life changed from CIDP to drinking, and that's a separate problem.

That's why, even though my last CIDP relapse was in 1999, I say I was sick for nine years.

Corroboration

I met a woman who took steroids for eleven years—thyroid cancer—and I asked her when she felt she had recovered.

She said she spent her thirties expecting to die of thyroid cancer and then turned forty. A year later she began a weight-loss program.

When she decided her obesity was a bigger problem than her cancer, she knew the cancer was over.

Having spent my twenties expecting to die, I turned thirty and arrived in the afterlife with nothing left to do. I wrote to an older friend, asking him what I should do now that I was thirty, having spent all my twenties expecting to die.

He wrote back that I should shoot for thirty-one.

Just Visiting

Here I am, eleven years after the day I woke with numb feet.

My friend Isabel is sitting in a blue plastic-upholstered easy chair with a twenty-two-gauge needle in her left arm. Her arm veins are good. She's receiving saline, steroids, and a designer immunosuppressant.

We're making off-color jokes. About sex, not death. There are some sick people on the other side of the curtain.

When I played Monopoly with my parents, when I was very young, we were careful to leave our playing pieces on the margins of the Jail square when we were Just Visiting.

I'm having a good time, just visiting. I feel like a secret guest of honor. I've taken more of everything than Isabel has. The nurses don't know it, but I do.

The nurse has just left, after connecting Isabel to a little glass jar, and we tell some more sex jokes, Isabel and me.

I'm sitting in a chair carried in from the waiting room. Isabel's in the center of the room, in the reclining armchair with the blue scallop shell print, with her left forearm resting on a pillow in a grayish white pillowcase, vein up, and with a grayish white blanket covering her bottom half.

We trade driver's licenses and make fun of the photographs and make more sex jokes. Isabel's infusion rate is increased, and she falls asleep.

Then she wakes up, a little euphoric, and we talk about drugs. Which ones we've done, which ones we're afraid to do, which ones we liked or didn't like. Which ones we're afraid might kill us. Then the death jokes start coming.

I'm having a good time, just visiting.

Memory

I argued with my father. He denied he'd read a book I lent him. In 1995 I watched him read it.

Later he wrote:

> *There are whole spans of time in the 1990s I don't remember.*
> *That's the only thing in my life that's like that.*

His tennis club later told him that in 1995 they watched him age a decade.

My mother wrote:

> *I don't remember the hospital sessions, but I remember the morning of the ambulance ride when you couldn't walk and I had to move you around on the desk chair. Never could explain to Nana about your disease. At the time she had the beginnings of Alzheimer's and would ask daily how you were, then have me explain. Every day, the same.*

Very isolated. Friends and family stayed away, perhaps in fear of catching the disease. Resented this but could understand.

When you were in the hospital I felt as if I had a little vacation because someone else was taking care of you.

Was always optimistic about your recovery. Guess that's my personality. Never was resentful but felt sad for you and often wondered why this had to happen.

Only had one friend who seemed genuinely interested, who I could talk with and who would visit both of us.

Now I remember the navy blue jacket my mother wore almost every day she visited me in the hospital.

I remember how angry I felt when my parents visited me at seven in the evening, when visiting hours were almost over, and when *My So-Called Life* was on television, so instead of having two things to do in a day, I had to choose one or the other.

I remember a long time later, seeing Claire Danes in a boutique on the Lower East Side and going in and telling her how much I'd liked watching *My So-Called Life*.

I remember that after an IV catheter in my arm got pulled out, I got infusions in my hand instead of my arm so I could keep a better eye on the tubes.

I remember meeting with my Latin professor and knowing he thought I was dying and not correcting him, and letting him tell me everything that would be on the exam.

I remember him conjugating a verb and saying *masculine and single* instead of *masculine and singular*, and how he blushed.

I remember my college boyfriend reading *Le Monde* in the Adams House dining hall and carrying Kierkegaard books in his pockets, and how they stuck out just enough that you could see it was Kierkegaard.

I remember learning the combination to the lock on the Fellows' liquor cabinet at the Signet, and feeling as good as I ever had, telling someone else the combination.

Relevance

If you could know anything about my disease, what would you want to know? Did it change me?

I don't know if it changed me. It happened in spacetime, which is a bad place to conduct a controlled experiment. Spacetime has too many variables already. It's not even a controlled experiment by itself.

I don't know if I changed because of my disease or in spite of it.

What if I don't mention the disease for eleven years? Was I thinking about it all that time? What if I talk about it constantly for eleven years? Am I avoiding thinking about something else?

Did anything important happen to me before the disease happened? After it happened? How important was the disease? More important than getting my driver's license? Having sex for the first time? Getting put in lockdown? What about when I moved to Iowa? What about when Victor died?

What about when I crashed my mother's car?

I am quite sure I crashed the car so everyone would see I wanted
to die. I wanted to die, but I didn't want to tell anyone. So I
took a left turn through a double lane of oncoming traffic,
only one lane of which I could see, and I hit a van full of kids.

Their mother came out laughing—was she laughing? Why
have I made her laugh in this memory? She knew I was at fault.
I knew I was at fault. And the police knew.

I think they also knew I wanted to die. I was a frail-looking
twenty-five-year-old woman driving an immaculate fifteen-
year-old black BMW sedan and I'd just hit a van full of kids,
and I knew I looked sedated but I couldn't help it, and the two
officers who came to the scene were very gentle with me.
They asked me if I were all right. I wanted to die, but I wasn't
hurt, so I said I was all right.

I could feel my face lying on top of my skull. I could feel it not
moving. I could feel my mouth move when I spoke, if I concentrated.

One of the officers explained very kindly that I was at fault by
definition, as I'd been the one turning into oncoming traffic. It
was all right. My mother's car was wrecked. I'd never been in a
wreck before. I wasn't concentrating on being in a wreck. I was
saving the wreck for later.

Then I went into the library, returned the books I'd brought to
return, stopped in the alcove, put a quarter into the pay phone,
and told my mother I'd been in an accident.

Then I drove home in the wrecked car. Did I drive home in the wrecked car? Or was it towed, and did someone pick me up and drive me home? I don't remember.

No, I do remember. I remember driving home in the wrecked sedan, but it had grown to the size of a Viking ship, and all other traffic had disappeared, and the roads had disappeared, and there was only me in my broken ship, floating home.

I wouldn't have to say a word. My friend Shane had just died. I could just have gone home in my broken ship, the ghost of my dead friend hovering above it, and everyone would know I wanted to die, too.

And the relevance of my disease would be obvious. Everyone would see that it was the culprit, that it was why I wanted to die.

I don't know how to write a novel. I like to ask writers who write novels how they do it. How they write something longer than what can be held in the eye comfortably, at middle distance.

How can I stop thinking about the disease long enough to write about anything else? How can I stop thinking about everything else long enough that I can write about the disease?

My friend Isabel says, *When you're writing even a short novel, with at least a couple of subplots, and God only knows how many characters, your brain holds the volume of it beyond the ability of your consciousness.*

Of course.

Measuring

A nine-year period began and ended.

I measure time by the movement of this planet. As any sane person would.

I tend to forget that my measurement of time is designed to distract me from what's really happening.

I tend to forget I'm walking on the surface of a soft mass on fire on the inside, a surface warmed and lit by an explosion taking place ninety-three million miles away. An explosion that started at some point and will end at some point.

I tend to forget that I rose out of this explosion and—despite my feeling I am unique from it—will someday fall back into it.

Why nine years?

Why do I need to read sixty minutes in the morning, and swim twenty laps in the afternoon, and write a thousand words at night, in order to feel that a twenty-four-hour period has been well used?

What are all these numbers for? What do they measure?

What do I think I'm clarifying by the act of measuring? What does measuring make *clearer*?

At the beginning there's conception, gestation, the growth of the brain in the womb. There's the crowning, the first breath, the naming.

At the end, unless you are vaporized in an explosion, the heart stops and the blood still moves in the veins, then the blood stops and the tissues still live, then the tissues die slowly, and at some point the last neuron in the brain dies. How long this takes depends on too many variables to measure.

My Jewish grandmother lived to be eighty-five. She thought she'd been born on December 10th, but when we found her birth certificate, it seemed she'd been born at home on the 8th or the 9th. There was snow in Boston, and the 10th was the first day anyone could get out to report the birth.

I have two letters she wrote to me at summer camp in the 1980s. One is dated *Tuesday 6/29*, and the other, *July 4—Happy Independence Day*.

What times aren't open to debate? What times are clear?

Wars end at particular times. They end when the document has been signed. They end at the first moment the document can be described as *signed*.

But it isn't so much that a war ends in a single moment as much as people decide to agree the war has ended in a single moment. And so the measurement becomes unassailable. Not accurate. Just unassailable.

Nothing happens in a moment. Nothing happens quickly. If you think something's happened quickly, you're looking at only a part of it.

Firing a rifle shot seems to happen quickly, but what about the movement of the trigger finger? What about the decision to fire the rifle? What about all your careful target practice? What about everything in your life that happened before you decide to fire that rifle?

How can you separate the incidental from what was necessary to your decision to pull the trigger?

Nothing happens in an instant. Nothing starts happening and nothing finishes happening. History doesn't begin anywhere. And it doesn't end.

Why is it important to me to know the beginning and end of this particular decay I think I'm writing about—which is just part of my own whole decay?

And couldn't the decay be called by many other names—for instance, my life?

The End

There are two kinds of decay: mine and everyone else's.

This is the usual sort of book about illness. Someone gets sick, someone gets well.

Those who claim to write about something larger and more significant than the self sometimes fail to comprehend the dimensions of a self.

Most people consider their own suffering a widely applicable model, and I am no exception.

This is suffering's lesson: *pay attention*. The important part might come in a form you do not recognize.

You might not know to love it.

But to pay attention is to love everything.

To see the future as *brightness*.

Everything that happens is the last time it happens. We see things only as their own fatal brightness, and there is nothing after that brightness.

You can't learn from remembering. You can't learn from guessing.

You can learn only from moving forward at the rate you are moved, as brightness, into brightness.